THE THOUGHT OF MIKHAIL BAKHTIN

D1253233

The Thought of Mikhail Bakhtin

From Word to Culture

David K. Danow

Associate Professor of Russian
University of California, Riverside

St. Martin's Press   New York

First published in the United States of America in 1991

Printed in Hong Kong

ISBN 0–312–05608–7 cloth
0–312–05609–5 paper

Library of Congress Cataloging-in-Publication Data
Danow, David K. (David Keevin), 1944–
    The thought of Mikhail Bakhtin : from word to culture / David K.
Danow.
        p.   cm.
    Includes bibliographical references and index.
    ISBN 0–312–05608–7 (hardcover). — ISBN 0–312–05609–5 (paperback)
    1. Bakhtin, M. M. (Mikhail Mikhaĭlovich), 1895–1975.
    2. Philology—History—20th century.   I. Title.
    P85.B22D3   1991
    801'.95'092—dc20
                                                    90–46988
                                                        CIP

For Mirjana,

My companion in life and dialogue

Contents

Part I

1

Bakhtin and His Circle

Nothing is absolutely dead: every meaning will have its
homecoming festival.
Bakhtin, 'Toward a Methodology for
the Human Sciences'

Mikhail Mikhailovich Bakhtin (1895–1975) is unquestionably one of the most important and influential literary
theoreticians and philosophers of language to emerge
from the starkly controlled ideological climate of Russia in
this century. His works devoted to Dostoevsky, Rabelais,
the novel form in general, whose attendant features in-
spired further investigations into problems of language in
narrative, and especially his writings on the dynamics of
dialogue, have had a great and rapidly increasing impact
upon a range of disciplines within the humanities, tran-
scending any single field among them.

Some two decades have passed since the star of Mikhail
Bakhtin began its phenomenal rise in the West. His difficult life and extraordinary career are documented in an
impressive, detailed literary biography that explores a
frequently confounding intellectual milieu, enshrouded
by the darkness of Stalin's impenetrable night (Clark and
Holquist 1984). As survivor of an earlier period in Russia,
when religious and theological matters might still be discussed, and as author of a number of strikingly original
works, which have come to deserved attention decades
after their initial publication, Bakhtin has emerged in
recent decades from virtual obscurity to remarkable
prominence as theorist of literature, language, and inter-
personal relations.

Occupying a still evolving but clearly established place
in twentieth-century intellectual history, Bakhtin is perhaps

3

best characterized as a philosopher of discourse or human communication. Tzvetan Todorov, a literary scholar who has brought much of contemporary Russian critical theory to the attention of the West, proclaims him 'the most important Soviet thinker in the human sciences and the greatest theoretician of literature in the twentieth century' (1984:ix). Wayne Booth, the American critic, asserts in similarly unequivocal terms that 'If Bakhtin is right, a very great deal of what we Western critics have spent our time on is mistaken, or trivial, or both' (*PDP*, xxv).[1] Subject to further critical assessment, in the ongoing effort to attain a circumspect judgment of Bakhtin and his achievement, such high acclaim came late and at great personal cost.

Remarkably, until some quarter of a century ago, Bakhtin was an obscure figure virtually unknown in his own homeland, let alone in the West. Legend has it that he was extremely cavalier about his writings, appearing unconcerned about their survival, or with who was ultimately credited with their authorship. But legend aside, he lived through six years of forced exile (1930–1936) from European Russia in Kazakhstan, at the outer limits of Central Asia, and suffered further great hardship in result of several more decades (1936–1972) of forced isolation from the cultural life of Moscow and Leningrad, which might also have afforded some semblance of material well-being (relative to the primitive conditions of Soviet provincial towns, uniformly condemned to basic hardship and extreme deprivation). All this was augmented further by the effects of a debilitating bone disease that earlier necessitated the amputation of a leg. Bakhtin was 'discovered' after Stalin's quarter-century-long night by a new generation of young literary scholars, who rescued his surviving manuscripts left to an uncertain fate in a woodshed in the Russian provincial town of Saransk. These students were also instrumental in retrieving other earlier works from continued obscurity by encouraging their author to revise and eventually see them into print.

Spanning more than half a century of extraordinary critical activity, Bakhtin's works were produced during a period blighted by the repressive Stalinist regime and the Second World War. That scholarly productivity is especially remarkable for its having been achieved in the face of dire Russian historical realities that confronted an entire generation: the Revolution and its aftermath, the institution of Marxist–Leninist dogma to the exclusion of other contending lines of religious or philosophical thought, the official dispersal of independent groups of scholars not conforming to the Party line. In the case of Bakhtin, years of exile very likely spared him a worse fate, suffered by others of his intellectual milieu, similarly guided by heterodox religious, literary, and philosophical views.

Perhaps no writer in the entire history of letters can lay claim to a more checkered literary career than Bakhtin. His book on Rabelais, with its attendant discussion of carnival, submitted as his doctoral dissertation in 1940, was not published until twenty-five years later, in 1965. His highly acclaimed work on Dostoevsky, proclaiming the great Russian writer a foremost practitioner of the 'polyphonic' novel, originally published in 1929, was revised, expanded, and finally republished in 1963, more than three decades after its original publication. One book-length manuscript was blown up, along with the publishing house to which it had been submitted, during the Second World War. In addition, several essays have been published posthumously, including those which have appeared in incomplete form, essentially as the author's notes.[2]

Beyond these textological concerns is the monumental fact that within a period of three years (1926–29), four now well-known and highly influential works appeared that have been associated with the name of Bakhtin, or directly attributed to him. These include *Problems of Dostoevsky's Art*, published under Bakhtin's own name (1929; republished with emendations in 1963, as *Problems of Dostoevsky's Poetics*); *Marxism and the Philosophy of Language* (1929) and *Freudianism: A Critical Sketch* (1927), both published as the work of V.N. Voloshinov; and *The Formal Method in Literary Scholarship* (1928), signed by P.N. Medvedev. Both

Voloshinov and Medvedev were compatriot thinkers (Voloshinov was a linguist, Medvedev a literary theorist), who were prominent members of the original Bakhtin 'circle', which flourished in the 1920s, affording a remarkably fruitful exchange of ideas on problems of language and literature.

That expression, partaking of a well-established historical tradition within the Russian cultural context, refers in this particularly productive instance to a group of intellectuals (whose membership shifted and changed with the passage of time), presided over by Bakhtin, which met regularly in the 1920s to discuss questions of science, religion, and art, before Stalin consolidated political control and drove certain of its members into exile and others into concentration camps, never to return.[3] The authorship of several of the works produced by members of the circle remains in dispute. Unresolved, and likely to remain so, the question inevitably resurfaces. Briefly formulated, it asks whether Bakhtin may have written – in whole or in part – works which do not carry his name, but certainly bear his imprint. Scholars on one side of the dispute argue for Bakhtin as author of (or greatest contributor to) several works not bearing his name, others require hard evidence (not yet forthcoming) before undertaking to remove the name of the putative author (Voloshinov or Medvedev) from a book or article, particularly after its having appeared there for well over half a century.

With respect to the writings that have emerged from that extraordinary intellectual milieu, we know that Bakhtin authored a major study of Dostoevsky and of Rabelais as well as a series of extensive essays devoted to philosophical and literary concerns, characterized by their profound entwinement. What we cannot affirm with any great certainty is the extent to which Bakhtin contributed (his ideas, writings, or own particular formulations?) to the so-called disputed texts. These include, most prominently, *Marxism and the Philosophy of Language*, heralded by some commentators as one of the best books on language to appear in this century; the book on Freudianism; and the study of the formal method, essentially a refutation of formalism. Theories abound as to why Bakhtin may have published his own works under the names of others. One hypothesis suggests that there might have been a greater likelihood of the books being published – given the strained political circumstances of Stalinist Russia in the 1920s – under 'pseudonyms' (of living persons nonetheless), perhaps affording a certain amount of political leverage (Bakhtin had none). Another theory posits that Bakhtin simply wanted to promote the careers of his friends and literary collaborators. Given what we know now, which may be all we will ever know of this strange and perplexing mystery, the question is not likely to be resolved through as yet undiscovered archival evidence, nor through irreproachable or indisputable oral confirmation. (The other two principals, Voloshinov and Medvedev, had both died by 1938.) Nevertheless, what is not subject to dispute is the fact that Bakhtin wrote several works in their entirety, and served as a guiding, formative influence on others, putatively authored by close associates.

Sketching the framework of Bakhtin's rich legacy, including the question of authorship, itself crucial to the resolution of greater theoretical issues, represents a textological question – perhaps the strangest of the century – to which specialists have been returning for the past fifteen years. A satisfactory answer, were one forthcoming, would afford us a clearer image of Bakhtin's individual thinking, philosophical positions, as well as evident biases. As a striking case of the latter, two careful readers of Bakhtin bluntly declare his 'lifelong dislike of Marxism' (Morson and Emerson 1989:2), asking, then, how Bakhtin could have possibly written – or even contributed, as guiding spirit, to – the monumental study *Marxism and the Philosophy of Language*? Turning that same question back on itself, others perceive the book as having little to do with Marxism in the first place. In any case, a clear determination of what Bakhtin did and did not write, would of necessity – as all the disputants agree – affect our entire assessment of what constitutes Bakhtin's *own* position. Further, a satisfactory textual resolution would also give us a better understanding of the same issues concerning Voloshinov and Medvedev, critical theorists in their own right. Part of the challenge for specialists in reading Bakhtin, then, is to be informed not only as to when a work was published, but also when it was written, as well as by whom, in an effort to determine the entire course of development of this intriguing body of thought.

There are at present essentially two points of view at odds regarding Bakhtin and his circle, centering in turn on two main concerns. The first questions the matter of authorship. The other focuses on whether Bakhtin wrestled with the same fundamental problems throughout his life, or whether they followed a certain organic development with 'new' concepts evolving from previous formulations. (The central problem of language, a fundamental case in point, may only have emerged at a median stage in Bakhtin's thought, argue Morson and Emerson.) At the core of the problem is the fact that the first question depends on further textological readings and comparisons, while the second will have to rely on some resolution to the first (which may never be wholly agreed upon). Until we can state with certainty what in fact Bakhtin wrote, in addition to what is already beyond doubt, or declare the exact nature of his contribution to other writings that have emerged from the extended philosophical discourse, which took place over years and in which Bakhtin played the leading role, we cannot attribute any sure line of development to what appears, in any case, a *collective* body of thought. No one, after all, questions whether there was scholarly collusion among the members of the circle – but only to what degree and to whom to attribute certain of the published manifestations resulting from that rich association.[4]

Published over a span of sixty years (1919–79), from a first brief essay to a posthumous collection of writings, several incomplete, Bakhtin's works do not elaborate a logical, philosophical system or cohesive, self-contained theory. Nor are they intended to, since Bakhtin rejected the whole idea of a prescribed system as detrimental to exploring what is singular about a given situation or individual. Under what he designates as 'theoretism', Bakhtin's argues against 'a way of thinking that abstracts from concrete human actions all that is generalizable, takes that abstraction as a whole, transforms the abstraction into a set of rules, and then derives norms from those rules' (Morson and Emerson 1989:7). For Bakhtin that is all wrong precisely because the individual event, with its unique contours, is swallowed whole by this inherently fallacious method of generalization.

Even less might a full-blown philosophical system or self-contained theory be derived from the varied and, indisputably, multi-authored body of thought acknowledged as the work of the Bakhtin circle. However, within that body there are repeatedly emphasized concerns that deserve to be isolated and analyzed, both on their own merits and in terms of their relation to one another, as fundamental components of an extended series of highly productive insights that promise further fruition in a number of related fields – including, among others, linguistics and semiotics, literary theory and poetics. It is from these linked perspectives that this study will approach its subject.

In doing so, the goal of the first part of this book is to provide a relatively unencumbered overview of several of the most significant aspects of Bakhtin's thought. Our intention is not to present a historical perspective but to offer a comprehensive summative viewpoint that remains as faithful as possible to the central issues and their essential formulation. This study is therefore designed with the aim to afford novitiate readers a brief but broadly encompassing introduction to a large and complex body of thought – riven, moreover, with more than its share of political as well as textological difficulties.

In acknowledging that Bakhtin's writings are non-systematic, our purpose will be to abstract and synthesize in the following three chapters several prominent features within a broad range of theoretical concerns. Beginning with Bakhtin's assumption that the word (or utterance) represents the foundation of all human communication, his essential preoccupation with that rich concept will occupy us in the next chapter. Bakhtin's views concerning the utterance in general and the word in particular range over the extended course of his writing as a subject of recurring interest, which is isolated and consolidated here.

Posited by Bakhtin at the other extreme, that same fundamental unit of communication – the utterance appearing as a single word – may also be manifested, paradoxically, as an entire text. The third chapter will therefore take up Bakhtin's understanding of the novel, regarded by him as the quintessential modern text. Most reflective of contending ideologies in a given time and place, the novel, as Bakhtin's preferred genre, is heralded as such for its unmatched attention to philosophic quest. Within a delimited framework, the utterance will thus be approached from possible manifestations as a single word to a fully developed work.

Bakhtin's lifelong concern with dialogic relations, embracing his thought in all areas, will serve as the unifying theme of these and other interrelated subjects treated here.[5] Nowhere does this most distinctive feature of his thought appear more prominently than in his discussion of the relations between what he conceived as the 'self and other', representing his most vital meaning-producing model of human communication. That model is the subject of chapter four.

The purpose of this study is in part to outline the thought of Bakhtin in terms of these briefly noted respects. That is essentially the work of the first part of the book, devoted to questions of language and literature. In addition, our aim is to discuss Bakhtin in relation to twentieth-century East European thought; specifically, to cite Bakhtin's preeminent role as precursor of the currently emerging study of the semiotics of culture, one of the most profitable directions taken by the doctrine of signs.[6] Accordingly, the second part of this study is designed as a set of related 'dialogues' between the thought of Bakhtin (as presented in the opening chapters) and that of the Prague Linguistic Circle, commonly referred to as the Prague School (1926–45), and the contemporary Moscow–Tartu School of Cultural Semiotics (1962–present) – both of which have claimed the study of culture as a principal subject of investigation.

Chapters five and six are therefore designed to explore the connections between the Bakhtin circle and these two prominent schools of thought, rooted both culturally and historically in related intellectual milieux. In establishing among them certain linkages as well as disparities in their respective thinking, the aim here is not to establish a hierarchy but to set forth the rich texture of their respective views, shared in certain instances, and precluded in others, that characterizes these several remarkable trends of thought – all the more so for their having been elaborated in times and places thoroughly blighted by the harsh political realities of the twentieth century.

Regarding the Prague School, itself most centrally concerned with problems of linguistics, the writings of Jan Mukařovský (1891–1975), its most important literary theoretician and aesthetician, will serve to represent its thought because of a range of interests that extends from language and literature to problems of culture. Nascent in him, such concerns were destined, paradoxically, to far greater development under an unsympathetic Soviet Communist regime some quarter of a century after the Prague School had been effectively silenced by Czechoslovakia's then like-minded political power. Thus, the (not yet fully appreciated) remarkable flowering of scholarly activity in Prague reemerged, after a long hiatus, in the Moscow–Tartu School, devoted for the last two decades to elaborating problems of the semiotics of culture. This reemergence took place in the Estonian capital of Tartu, under the tutelage of Yury Lotman, as well as in Moscow, through the common effort of other Russian scholars of diverse backgrounds, all of whom shared an interest in the potential for a revived study of sign theory. While the School has been heralded worldwide for its extraordinary achievements in launching a discipline devoted to this new field, still in an inchoate stage of development, it has been greeted with little political favor at home.

In discussing the School (many of whose original members have since emigrated from the Soviet Union), the thought of no single figure has been extensively isolated (although Lotman and Boris Uspensky figure most prominently), at least in part because many of its writings constitute joint efforts on the part of the School's original members. Nonetheless, Lotman himself is commonly acknowledged by both past and present members of the School – as well as by the scholarly community at large – as being not only its historical founder but its principal energizing source. While particular attention is frequently paid to Mukařovský (because of his broad interests in literature and the arts) as a singular member of the Prague School, Lotman figures as the leading representative of a still flourishing intellectual trend, itself vitalized by diverse interests and disciplines.

In an effort to highlight frequent points of commonality as well as elements of divergence between Bakhtin and these two important schools of thought, the related concepts of monologue and dialogue, and of the word in relation to the artistic work, will be discussed in chapter five, drawing upon the thought of both the Prague School and the Bakhtin circle, in an effort to proceed from a concentration upon the word as microcosm, to related concepts of text and culture as extended macrocosm. A similar dialogue is proposed in chapter six between certain areas of thought characteristic of Bakhtin and others specifically related to the Moscow–Tartu School. Certainly the School has acknowledged Bakhtin as a noteworthy predecessor, as testified by numerous references.[7] Our aim there will be to establish certain correlations regarding the concept of the 'frame' in verbal art, as well as to explore a like set of analogies between Bakhtin's views on the novel in relation to the School's similar emphases concerning its concept of culture. Interestingly, what the School says about culture corresponds to Bakhtin's idea of the novel. While our concern is not to preside over the appropriation of one line of thought by another, there are nonetheless similarities as well as disparities in points of view that deserve attention as significant to contemporary twentieth-century Russian thought.

As the fundament of his project, Bakhtin proposes in his remarkable book on Dostoevsky a new scholarly discipline termed 'translinguistics', intended as the study of concrete dialogic exchange. In this all-encompassing respect, his thought embraces not only the linked realms of both everyday and literary discourse but also ethical and meta-physical concerns, encompassed by the diametrically opposed positions of 'dialogism' in relation to 'monologism'. The aim of the final chapter will be to assess this fundamental opposition, which, in effect, promotes a move from poetics to politics.

*

In a late essay devoted to 'The Problem of Speech Genres', Bakhtin takes up his lifelong concern with what he termed 'living speech', by arguing that there are typical forms of utterances that constitute entire speech genres. In contrast to literary and rhetorical genres, but like the utterance *per se*, these forms have not been paid due attention. Yet their importance is underscored by the fact that 'We are given these speech genres in almost the same way that we are given our native language, which we master fluently long before we begin to study grammar'. Speech genre acquisition is thus highly analogous to language acquisition. 'The forms of language and the typical forms of utterances, that is, speech genres, enter our experience and our consciousness together, and in close connection with one another. Speech genres organize our speech in almost the same way as grammatical (syntactical) forms do' (*SG*, 78–9). Just as the individual absorbs a language with its highly complex grammatical strictures seemingly effortlessly, so does a person discriminate among various complexes of typical utterances, or speech genres, in choosing not simply an adequate lexicon but a similarly apt mode of expression.

Arguing thus, Bakhtin challenges the entire field of linguistics to revise its basic mode of approach and get beyond static grammatical concerns to the more dynamic dialogic basis of all human communication. In calling into question the purpose of linguistics, he proclaims a fundamental distinction between the sentence which he views as a unit of language and the utterance which he conceives as the basic unit of speech communication. He charges that such concepts as 'the mythical' (supposedly natural) 'speech flow' must be rejected in favor of a study of the utterance. Linguists, in his view, 'see in the utterance only an individual combination of purely linguistic (lexical and grammatical) forms and they neither uncover nor study any of the other normative forms the utterance acquires in practice' (*SG*, 81). Central here is Bakhtin's repeated argument that linguistics must focus upon language in common practical usage, rather than in isolated theoretical possibility.

In distinguishing between the sentence as a unit of language and the utterance as a unit of speech, Bakhtin concludes that the utterance is the basis of human communication. 'The sentence as a language unit is grammatical in nature. It has grammatical boundaries and grammatical completedness and unity' (*SG*, 74). Whereas the sentence is perceived thus as a grammatically organized entity, the utterance is viewed as an ideologically governed structure, designed to express fully a particular responsive position. The former affords the finality of an element, the latter allows for the finalization of the whole. In this important sense, the utterance alone is complete, and therefore suited to further linguistic study. As a clearly evident exception to such juxtaposition, when a single sentence constitutes a speaker's entire response, it necessarily coincides with Bakhtin's understanding of the utterance. Bakhtin also affirms that the utterance may be equated with an interjection (or sigh), as one possible mode of dialogic response, but may also be conceivably manifested as an entire text (specifically the novel). A concept that embraces virtually the whole range of human verbal communication must at least call for some pause. Should not the concept be delimited in some way? Would such delimitation (that is, more precise definition) reduce or increase its effectiveness as an analytical tool? In proclaiming such wide-ranging applicability, Bakhtin's project calls for certain modification. This issue is taken up more broadly in chapter seven, whose focus is extended to encompass that entire project under the name of dialogism, which makes its own set of expansive claims and bears similar attendant problems.

The definitive aspect of completeness that Bakhtin declares inherent in the utterance is assured, in his view, by the speaker's 'speech plan' or 'speech will', which also determines its length and boundaries. In result, 'The boundaries of each concrete utterance as a unit of speech communication are determined by a *change of speaking subjects*' (*SG*, 71), meaning that the alternation of speakers affords the clear-cut boundaries that distinctly frame each utterance. Hence dialogue may be understood, in this limited traditional sense, as alternating monologue. Each utterance, clearly demarcated by its articulating voice, contributes to the ongoing, never ending dialogue. Bakhtin emphasizes the motivating dialogical aspect of the utterance when he repeatedly proclaims that 'Any utterance is a link in a very complexly organized chain of other utterances. . . . Any utterance is a link in the chain of speech communion'. Filled with *'dialogic overtones'*, such structure – although complete – is never isolated; rather, it is always responsive (*SG*, 69, 84, 92). Thus Bakhtin argues that an inherent propensity towards dialogue is a distinctive property of language.

In addition, the speaker's 'speech will' determines the choice of a particular speech genre, understood as corresponding to 'typical situations of speech communication, typical themes, and, consequently, also to particular contacts between the *meanings* of words and actual concrete reality under typical circumstances' (*SG*, 87). In other words, depending upon the situation, a specific mode of address and corresponding level of speech is chosen to convey one message as opposed to another. Certain speech genres, however, are conceived as more standardized than others, including, for example, such basic amenities as an exchange of greetings. Thus, Bakhtin affirms, on the one hand, the distinctive role of the speaker in choosing a given strategy by which to communicate. But at the same time that speaker is confronted by a plethora of speech genres that act, in effect, as constraints, much as the grammar of a language does on the most basic level of human communication. Likewise, on a more complex plane (where grammatical rules are embedded within generic norms), similar constraints apply in the way the writer must work within certain modes of established literary tradition.

While obliged to communicate within the framework of such constraints, the speaker retains as part of a nonetheless varied and extensive repertoire the ability to express his emotionally evaluative attitude toward the referent (or subject) by means of expressive intonation. For Bakhtin, there can be no such thing as an absolutely neutral utterance. The possibility of neutrality is consistently countered or negated by the speaker effecting a deliberately chosen intonation that belongs to the utterance as a constitutive, defining feature. In fact, there are instances when the semantic plane of the word (its commonly accepted meaning) is subordinated to a particular desired intonation, designed as the predominant strategy in making a point.

As a further constraint or partially determining factor, 'An essential (constitutive) marker of the utterance is its quality of being directed to someone, its *addressivity*'. Bakhtin thus affirms, in conformity with basic semiotic thought, that each utterance has both an author, who affords it a particularized intonation and mode of expression, and an addressee, who also contributes to its formulation. 'Each speech genre in each area of speech communication has its own typical conception of the addressee, and this defines it as a genre. . . . Addressivity, the quality of turning to someone, is a constitutive feature of the utterance; without it the utterance does not and cannot exist' (*SG*, 95, 99). Hence the utterance is defined by these constitutive features: its framed aspect, resulting in its specific finalization, and 'the relation of the utterance to the *speaker himself* (the author of the utterance) and to the *other* participants in speech communication' (*SG*, 84). The utterance is framed and thus finalized by the speaker, who chooses whatever speech genre is most suited to the intended message. In addition, the speaker communicates through expressive intonation his attitude toward the message and toward the addressee, whose recognition and anticipated participation in dialogue further determines the mode of speech or particular genre employed.

In the alternation of speech segments each speaker's utterance is bounded by the responsive utterance of his interlocutor. However, the utterance is finalized by the intent and will of the speaker, who presumably is allowed to complete the message before the other responds. By contrast, a single sentence will constitute only a part of the speaker's intent. In principle only a fragment of a given utterance, the sentence is a grammatical construct without orientation, while the utterance as an area worthy of linguistic consideration bears an orientation that takes into account both the speaker's relation to the message and to the addressee. An utterance as a whole is thus directed toward the other, whose overall intent and prior utterances determine in part the utterance of the present speaker. The latter in turn modifies a previously stated point of view as part of his strategy effectively to convince the other. It is these dynamics, in Bakhtin's view, that linguistics ignores by concentrating on units of language (from phoneme to sentence), rather than on the utterance as the unit of speech communication.

In proclaiming this failing on the part of linguistics, Bakhtin's arguments are frequently cast within the framework of such oppositions as openness versus closure or a finalized as opposed to an unfinalized event.[8] Whereas he generally favors unboundedness and incompletion, as in the generic case of the novel, for instance (or in allowing for the ongoing dialogue to continue on the grand metaphysical plane), in his discussion of the utterance, by contrast, Bakhtin valorizes its framed aspect and finalized quality as being able to render meaning beyond more limited grammatical constructs. The fact that the utterance is both framed (by other utterances) and finalized (by the speaker's intent) affords it a particular expressive quality or intonational component – oriented toward the addressee – that is lacking in the sentence and that therefore warrants greater attention than linguistics has so far been able to show.

*

As a prominent manifestation of the utterance, Bakhtin's concept of the word as a specific dialogical construct, intentionally and strategically deployed, deserves elaboration within a unified view abstracted from the whole range of works and subjects attributed to him. The Russian term *slovo* affords a logical point of departure. While it may be translated as either 'word' or 'discourse', the two are essentially interchangeable, since a single word may in a given situation represent an entire discourse bearing its own ideology, intent, or special meaning. Accordingly, Bakhtin perceives the word as dramatically engaged in continuous ideological dispute, affording the potential for further dialogue and greater understanding.

From one affirming perspective, Bakhtin's 'conception of the "literary word"' is heralded 'as an *intersection of textual surfaces* rather than a *point* (a fixed meaning), as a dialogue among several writings: that of the writer, the addressee (or the character), and the contemporary or earlier cultural context' (Kristeva 1980:65). While that observation attempts to cover a large semantic field with a single formulation (requiring certain qualification), it nevertheless serves to demonstrate the need for further elaboration of Bakhtin's rich concept of the Word.

Another like positive viewpoint asserts that Bakhtin's concept 'incorporates both the meaning of the word as a lexical unit and a more general meaning of verbal activity, the verbal aspect of human life. . . . By including into *slovo* all the gamut of secondary association, contextual meanings and behavioral accompaniments, Bakhtin broadened its function and sphere and made the word transcend its purely linguistic borders' (Segal 1974:124). It is this 'transcendence' that will interest us here.

That the concept of the word is of critical importance not only to Bakhtin's translinguistics but also to his metaphysics is made evident in a statement written near the end of his life: 'I live in a world of others' words. And my entire life is an orientation in this world, a reaction to others' words . . . beginning with my assimilation of them . . . and ending with assimilation of the wealth of human culture' (*SG*, 143). Thus, when Bakhtin writes,

'There is an ancient tie between the feast and the spoken word' (*RW*, 283), it becomes evident that the 'feast' is indeed an extensive one – encompassing all of human culture. In this study, that figurative 'ancient tie' will be explored, beginning with the word and ending with the feast. Within that broadly encompassing sphere, there is, for Bakhtin, a natural progression, originating with the word, proceeding to the utterance, and concluding with the text (itself constituting a potential new point of departure). For a single word may represent an entire utterance in a given context and a single utterance may likewise figure as a complete text.[9] As the fundamental component of an utterance, the word is the principal source of the text, itself the primary manifestation and main ideological constituent of culture. The word *is* the beginning in the theology of Bakhtin. And culture is the end, the primary goal of the word.

2
Bakhtin's Concept of the Word

> . . . nothing conclusive has yet taken place in the world,
> the ultimate word of the world and about the world has
> not yet been spoken, the world is open and free, every-
> thing is still in the future and will always be in the
> future.
>
> Bakhtin, *Problems of Dostoevsky's Poetics*

In declaring the need for a new discipline devoted to the
study of dialogic relations, Bakhtin outlines an approach
to the word in narrative which concentrates upon language
as articulated utterance, rather than upon the potential for
communication that language bears in the abstract. Rendered as 'translinguistics' (or less suitably as 'metalinguis-
tics'), this proposed field of study intends to tackle
problems which are considered beyond the ken of traditional linguistics – 'the study of those aspects in the life of
the word, not yet shaped into separate and specific disciplines' (*PDP*, 181). Primary among such problems is the
concrete usage of language in both everyday speech and
literary discourse, within whose range is afforded the
dynamic potential for dialogue. As its main tenet, this new
discipline is founded on the principle that an immanent
propensity toward dialogue or verbal exchange is a definitive feature of language.

While firmly rooted in a stated emphasis upon the
concrete, just how broadly inclusive this proposed field
might be appears evident upon consideration of the
sweeping affirmation that 'Any true understanding is
dialogic in nature' (*MPL*, 102). In this same all-
encompassing spirit, it is proclaimed that 'no distinct or

21

clear consciousness of the world is possible outside of the word' (*FM*, 133). However broad and unqualified, these linked affirmations (asserted by Bakhtin's two fellow theorists, respectively) are at the core of Bakhtin's thought. For in their linkage, the preeminent importance of dialogue, as the exclusive means to understanding, is paralleled by the word, which is privileged not only as the principal means of communication between individuals engaged in dialogic exchange but as the exclusive mode for apprehending and interpreting the world and all of its objects. Hence the task of Bakhtin's projected discipline is to explore the dynamic interrelations between the word of the 'self and other' in a 'concrete living context' (*PDP*, 199), delimited only by the potential for dialogic understanding.

Traditional linguistics, for Bakhtin, is narrowly concerned with the word as a static lexical element having a certain object or referent. Within the broader conceptual framework which Bakhtin proposes, however, the word is conceived as an utterance invested with a distinct significance and meaning, whose definitive features are its communicative aspect and intent. These enable it to transcend its purely logical or concrete semantic relationships and enter into the dialogical relationships which afford it specificity. In this view, not only does the subject lend specificity to his utterance, but so does another's reaction, another's word – the two 'interpenetrating' the single utterance, establishing, as a result, its specific locus of meaning. The word in such cases cannot be relegated to the level of lexical item, since another's 'voice' (or intention) can be detected in that word. If within a single word or utterance there are distinguished two voices, that utterance is understood to embody a dialogical relationship, since 'a dialogic approach is possible toward any signifying part of an utterance, even toward an individual word, if that word is perceived not as the impersonal word of language but as a sign of someone else's semantic position . . .' That is, it is understood to incorporate 'a relationship to someone else's utterance as an indispensable element . . .' (*PDP*, 184, 186) within one's own utterance.

Upon this understanding dialogic relations may be provisionally defined as encompassing the speaker's 'present' utterances, both his own previous and possible future statements, and those (past and future) of his interlocutor – since 'An element of response and anticipation penetrates deeply inside intensely dialogic discourse' (*PDP*, 197). This same model applies as well to a single individual engaged in thought (or 'inner speech', as Bakhtin would have it), in which case the dialogic relations of the speaker to his own utterances are conceived as 'limiting our own authorship or dividing it in two' (*PDP*, 184), as when a speaker hesitates, revealing an inner reservation. Or, as Bakhtin puts it elsewhere, emphasizing this time the relation between the speaker as both subject and 'object': 'By objectifying myself . . . I gain the opportunity to have an authentically dialogic relationship with myself' (*SG*, 122). In this view, no clear distinction is made between inner and outwardly manifested speech: both are seen as the product and expression of dialogic interaction. The other, in other words, may be oneself (and most frequently is) – but that 'other' is also understood to be an *ever changing* self.

Essentially the same idea finds its concise formulation in the writings of the American logician and semiotician, Charles Sanders Peirce, who claims that 'thinking always proceeds in the form of a dialogue – a dialogue between different phases of the ego . . .' (1933:4.6). Even more succinctly, Peirce observes: 'All thinking is dialogic in form' (1935:6.338), a premise with which Bakhtin would surely agree. A special emphasis emerges, however, when Bakhtin proclaims that dialogic relations 'lie in the realm of discourse for discourse is by its very nature dialogic' (*PDP*, 183). Accordingly, dialogue is perceived as immanent to language as the basis of all human communication. Formulated repeatedly in an unequivocal manner, that view asserts that 'verbal interaction is the basic reality of language' (*MPL*, 94) and that dialogue is 'the most natural form of language' (Voloshinov, *BSP*, 117).

What allows for such unequivocal formulation is the attendant understanding of the word and its function. The word, first of all, is understood as being dialogical, since it takes cognizance of another speaker's word perhaps even prior to or at the very moment of utterance. It is conceived as a sign not only bearing meaning, or having a referent, but as being potentially engaged in continuous dialogue. This concept of the dialogic word applies to all spheres of communication (including 'inner' as well as outer speech). But as a diametrically opposed position, the possibility of monological utterance is manifested in one sense when an 'author's word' is perceived as consciously and intentionally claiming a seemingly indisputable authority. 'One who creates a direct word – whether epic, tragic, or lyric – deals only with the subject whose praises he sings, or represents, or expresses, and he does so in his own language that is perceived as the sole and fully adequate tool for realizing the word's direct, objectivized meaning' (*DI*, 61). In this sense, dialogue is precluded.

Opposed, then, to the several manifestations of the 'double-voiced' word is the 'single-voiced' word, which, in contrast to the former, does not take into account another speaker's utterance but focuses solely on the object of speech. As such, it represents the subject of traditional stylistic and linguistic approaches to the lexical item, which 'recognize only the direct unmediated orientation of discourse toward its referential object, without taking into account anyone else's discourse or any second context' (*PDP*, 186). Such a word 'is indissolubly fused with its authority – with political power, an institution, a person – and it stands and falls together with that authority. . . . It is by its very nature incapable of being double-voiced . . . If completely deprived of its authority it becomes simply an object, a *relic*, a *thing*' (*DI*, 343, 344). This, in effect, constitutes the 'authoritarian word' – one that does not permit any other to oppose it or offer any qualification or emendation.

In this line of thought, there are no 'neutral' words which 'belong to "no one"' (*DI*, 293), since this would be tantamount to asserting that there are (dictionary) words which have never been used by anyone. On the other hand, although the word itself is not deemed neutral, it is regarded as a neutral sign, since 'It can carry out ideological functions of any kind – scientific, aesthetic, ethical, religious' (*MPL*, 14). Bakhtin is therefore able to declare that 'language has been completely taken over, shot through with intentions and accents. . . . Each word tastes of the context and contexts in which it has lived its socially charged life; all words and forms are populated by intentions. Contextual overtones . . . are inevitable in the word' (*DI*, 293). All words, moreover, are attributable to a particular profession or group, a certain level of society, a generation, a historical period. In short, to extend a thoroughly proliferated anthropomorphic analogy in Bakhtin's writings, the word – like its users – lives a life of its own, and is likewise affected by other words. As Bakhtin suggests, the word will therefore 'taste' of certain associations inherent within it and may be made to imply such bonds through the user's strategic employment of it.

Within the context of the novel, such discourse is termed 'heteroglossia', defined as *'another's speech in another's language*, serving to express authorial intentions but in a refracted way. Such speech constitutes a special type of double-voiced discourse' (*DI*, 324), in which there are always present two voices and two meanings, and which is therefore always internally dialogized. In a broader sense, the term refers to the multiple connotations a word bears by virtue of its association with some ideological position, social or political group, or single individual. The notion of heteroglossia, in effect, represents the positive correlative to the idea that no word is neutral, and that 'no word belongs to no one'; for the converse asserts that every word belongs to someone, who, having used it in a certain context, has imbued it with a special sense peculiar to that context. In time, the word becomes identified with all such contextual residue.

In the case of narrative, this feature of language may be utilized by the author to express in oblique fashion intentions of his own, while purporting to convey those of his character. That both the character's and author's intentions belong ultimately to the latter as creator of his verbal universe raises an apparent contradiction. However,

Bakhtin is arguing for the 'freedom' of the character 'within the limits of the artistic design' (*PDP*, 64), and in this sense, the two viewpoints of author and character need not coincide. Of greater importance, another's discourse in general is seen to represent a largely unrecognized but main topic of discourse itself in both verbal art and in life (*DI*, 337–42). The artistic representation of another's speech and intention therefore constitutes a central problem of prose theory. How such transmission of another's speech is accomplished is seen as crucial to the study of narrative (*MPL*, 109–59), where the double-voiced, internally dialogized word, in all its diverse forms, requires further exploration and elucidation. As Bakhtin repeatedly declares: 'an investigation of discourse from the point of view of its relationship to someone else's discourse, has . . . exceptionally great significance for an understanding of artistic prose' (*PDP*, 199–200). This significance and the sense of the 'inner life' of the word is communicated thus:

> The word is not a material thing, but rather the eternally mobile, eternally changing medium of dialogic interaction. It never gravitates toward a single consciousness or a single voice. The life of the word is contained in its transfer from one mouth to another, from one context to another context, from one social collective to another, from one generation to another generation. In this process the word does not forget its own path and cannot completely free itself from the power of these concrete contexts into which it has entered.

> When a member of a speaking collective comes upon a word, it is not as a neutral word of language, not as a word free from the aspirations and evaluations of others, uninhabited by others' voices. No, he receives the word from another's voice and filled with that other voice. The word enters his context from another context, permeated with the interpretation of others. His own thought finds the word already inhabited. Therefore the orientation of the word among words, the

varying perception of another's word and the various means for reacting to it, are perhaps the most fundamental problems for the metalinguistic study of any kind of discourse, including the artistic (*PDP*, 202).

In Bakhtin's writings there are frequent references to a whole spectrum of 'words' of various hues and shadings. His reader encounters detailed considerations of the 'single-voiced' contrasted to the 'double-voiced word'; the 'object-oriented' and 'objectified word' as opposed to various forms of stylized language; the 'direct word' juxtaposed to the 'parodistic word'; one's 'own word' as opposed to another's 'alien word'; the 'novelistic word', the 'authoritarian word', the 'laughing word', the 'internally persuasive word', the 'new word', and numerous other specifications and sub-categories – all of which may be appropriated under a rubric specifying either a monologic utilization of the word or its dialogic usage. Bakhtin's noted study of Dostoevsky is largely concerned with elaborating the latter (in contrast to the former), which he broadly terms a 'polyphonic' approach to language and literature, but which also finds its more extended expression in the term 'dialogism'.

DISCOURSE TYPOLOGY

As the fundamental opposition between these various categories of the word, Bakhtin opposes its single-voiced, monologic expression to its double-voiced, dialogic mode. The former represents the direct referential speech of a single individual expressing an authoritative point of view. It specifies, informs, and is oriented toward its referent or words within the same context or the same speech. Within this first rubric, Bakhtin specifies two sub-categories: the object-oriented, as opposed to the objectified (or objectivized) word. While both forms focus upon the referent or upon related utterances within the same context, the first represents the author's word or dominant mode of expression. The latter belongs to the character as his representative word, which is 'meant to be understood not only from the point of view of its own referential object, but is itself, as characteristic, typical, colorful discourse, a referential object toward which something is directed' (*PDP*, 186–7). In other words, the word may serve as a sign of the speaker – ostensibly chosen to reflect a characteristic feature of that speaker. While the object-oriented (authorial) word predominates with its intention over the (character's) objectified word, it does not incorporate the latter unto itself with its own perspective or intentions. Rather, it allows it a separate existence but one which 'unwittingly', as it were, serves the author's overall purpose, while itself ostensibly serving to express the particular (although subordinate) individual perspective of its user, whom it also represents, significantly, as a sign.

By contrast with the single-voiced word in either of its two noted manifestations, the double-voiced word is inherently dialogic, since the writer makes use of another's word – already permeated with an initial, original intent – by incorporating his own specific intentions within it. This kind of utterance thus bears a dual burden of intent: that of the original 'speaker' and that of the writer who injects into it his own (opposing, supportive, ironic, or travestied) meaning, in which case 'two semantic intentions appear, two voices' (*PDP*, 189) are present in a single discourse. Within this category, Bakhtin specifies a number of types, 'hybrids' and sub-categories, exhibiting varying degrees of 'single-directedness' and 'heterodirectedness' (the latter indicating virtual reciprocity or mutual penetration of intentions) as well as a varying orientation toward another speaker's word. This latter feature essentially specifies and defines the basic concept of the double-voiced word.

From within this complex typology, in which these schematic categories are not mutually exclusive but merge and overlap, two opposing types will serve to illustrate the distinction between the single-directed and heterodirected mode (within the entire range of the double-voiced word): stylization (in various forms) contrasted

with the parodistic word. In the first instance, 'by inserting a new semantic intention into a discourse which already
has, and which retains, an intention of its own' (*PDP*,
189), the writer 'grafts' his intent upon the original, but
does not change its initial semantic thrust or direction. The
effect of the writer's additional, new emphasis is to make
the other's word conditional – in the sense that it loses its
absolute (single-voiced) authority and independence.
Analogous to such usage is the writer's employment of a
narrator to tell what is, after all, his story. In effect, the
author's usage of another's word as stylization serves to
weaken or make it less authoritative, yet the essential,
original intent remains fundamentally unchanged.

On the other hand, the use of another's word to establish mutually opposed and exclusive ends defines the
parodistic word, where the writer employs the utterance
of another for entirely different and contradictory purposes than originally intended. 'As in stylization, the
author again speaks in someone else's discourse, but in
contrast to stylization parody introduces into that discourse a semantic intention that is directly opposed to the
original one.' With proclaimed emphasis upon the concrete, Bakhtin's formulations are nevertheless frequently
figurative: the word is 'alive' but constantly at ideological
'war' as well. 'Discourse', we read, 'becomes an arena of
battle between two voices [that] are not only isolated from
one another . . . but are also hostilely opposed' (*PDP*,
193). In effect, it is that 'arena' which most consistently
concerns Bakhtin, whose principal aim is to show that in
daily speech as well as in narrative the word is engaged in
a constant struggle to express an ideology (belonging to its
user) that is being continuously formulated, subsequently
opposed by the word of the other, and consequently
reformulated.

In sum, the concept of the single-voiced word is intended to be representative of a given work's dominant,
authoritative mode of expression. As the object-oriented
type, it belongs to the author; as the objectified form, it is
attributed to a character, whose utterances are in any case
subordinated to the author's own strict intent. In contrast,

the double-voiced word refers to that ostensibly belonging to another but utilized by the author in a new distinctive way. This is accomplished through the word's contextual appropriation, stylized usage, or parody. Such strategies allow the author to 'penetrate' the word (of the other) with his own highly specific aims and intent, making it conform to *his* goals and orientation, whether they essentially coincide with the (other's) original intent, thus allowing for the writer's stylization of it – or are diametrically opposed, requiring his parodic utilization instead.

As the final opposition in Bakhtin's typology of the word in narrative, he juxtaposes the author's appropriation of it as a passive entity, on the one hand, with its being directly reacted to as an active, determining force, on the other. He considers that the first two types of the double-voiced word – represented here in the opposition between stylization and parody – allow for a utilization of the other person's word which is viewed as a 'completely passive tool in the hands of the author, [who] takes, so to speak, someone else's meek and defenseless discourse and installs his own interpretation in it, forcing it to serve his own new purposes' (*PDP*, 197).

Polemical strategies, by contrast, are seen to be activated by the author's particular awareness of another (potential) utterance. In this case, the other's speech – or presumed intentions – determine in some measure the otherwise solely object-oriented word of the author. Reference within this final category to only a single generic instance – the 'word with a sideward glance' – will serve to sum up the idea. In this case, the author is presumed to reflect – and act – upon the possible, or already completed, articulation of a potentially 'hostile' word. 'Such speech literally [sic!] cringes in the presence or anticipation of someone else's word, reply, objection.' This consideration influences and to a certain degree determines the writer's own utterance, since he is at the same time attempting to take into account the other's intention. In fact, Bakhtin claims that in every prose style there is an element of 'internal polemic' expressed to some degree. 'Every literary discourse more or less sharply senses its own listener, reader, critic, and reflects in itself their anticipated objections, evaluations, points of view' (*PDP*, 196). This is universally the case. For the word in narrative inevitably bears a 'loophole' which affords the opportunity for a 'sideward glance' at the word of the other. The same might be said of the word in everyday discourse as well.

It is the task of Bakhtin's projected translinguistics to assess and contrast the dynamic interrelations between one's own (or the author's) word and the utterance of another 'in a concrete living context'. To this end he establishes relevant typologies to pursue and extend the analysis of the double-voiced (dialogical) word initiated in his study of the word (or discourse) in Dostoevsky. In its broadest lineaments, Bakhtin's discourse typology is organized, first, according to whether or not a given utterance registers the existence of some other utterance (that is, whether it is single- or double-voiced); second, according to whether that registration is uni-directional or reciprocal; and, finally, at a deeper level of analysis, in terms of such critical relations between utterances as stylization, parody, and polemic. Yet the boundaries among these categories are fluid, rather than fixed, allowing for the merging of several possibilities within any given instance.

THE WORD AS SIGN

Bakhtin considers that the word is in a state of perpetual interaction. He consistently grants it an aggressive character as an entity struggling in the world to make itself heard within the unceasing global polemic, in which each voice attempts to convince with its particular world view.

The word, directed toward its object, enters a dialogically agitated and tension-filled environment of alien words, value judgments and accents, weaves in and out of complex interrelationships, merges with some, recoils from others, intersects with yet a third group: and all this may crucially shape discourse, may leave a trace in all its semantic layers, may complicate its expression and influence its entire stylistic profile (*DI*, 276).

The word is thus engaged in a constant struggle to achieve meaning and influence. Bakhtin's distinction between one's 'own word' and the 'alien word' of the other is especially crucial, since the latter is of necessity assimilated and incorporated as part of the former. Just as one cannot invent a language of one's own as a means of expression (and expect to be understood), one does not utilize the language commonly available in a purely individualized sense. Rather, language previously employed by others is utilized to suit best one's present purposes, thereby making the contextually appropriate contribution to the 'encrustation of meanings' (*DI*, 432; ed.) which has accrued to that word and which, in turn, inevitably affects the present intention of its user. Bakhtin can therefore wryly claim: 'words have "conditions attached to them"': it is not strictly speaking, *I* who speak; I, perhaps, would speak quite differently' (*DI*, 65). The same is expressed in the converse: 'Only the mythical Adam, who approached a virginal and as yet verbally unqualified world with the first word, could really have escaped from start to finish this dialogic interorientation with the alien word that occurs in the object' (*DI*, 279). In making reference to some aspect of the world, the word is already bonded to the previous 'alien' references of others, and is therefore obliged to make felt its distinctive concerns and individualized perspective. To this end, it must 'penetrate' the object with its own intention, permeating it temporarily with a new meaning born of a unique and unrepeatable context.

Similarly, the manifold contexts in which the word is given concrete meaning are also seen to be 'in a state of constant tension, or incessant interaction and conflict' (*MPL*, 80). No context is ever quite the same as another. It follows, therefore, that any utilization of the word within a given context must also be unique. Yet at the same time it is presumed that there inheres in both the word and its corresponding object an infinitely open-ended series of meanings, affording, with each contextual usage, a potentially new sense. Hence we find the extreme formulation: 'The meaning of a word is determined entirely by its context' (*MPL*, 79). Clearly requiring modification, this conception of the word heralds it as being wholly contextually dependent and therefore the bearer of a potential multiplicity of meanings. Yet it also conceives of the word and its object as perpetually unfinished constructs, to which additions and emendations can always be made. This feature of 'unfinishedness' is regarded by Bakhtin as entirely positive. For what is never completed may be further elaborated in a never-ending creative process, whose goal is further dialogue, from which accrues additional, deeper meaning (as expressed in the affirming spirit of the epigraph to the present chapter).

In a crucial respect the word is conceived figuratively as stratified and interpenetrated throughout with the past contextual meanings and intentions of the other. But in another, concrete sense, the word is conceived as a thing of substance: 'Whatever a word might mean, it is first of all materially present, as a thing uttered, written, printed, whispered, or thought. . . . [It] is always an objectively present part of man's social environment' (*FM*, 8). The 'material presence of the word' is affirmed as well by the fact that 'Every concrete utterance is . . . an individual material complex, a phonetic, articulatory, verbal complex . . .' (*FM*, 119, 120). But as complementary consideration to the word as 'thing', in verbal art the word is also conceived as the image of what it represents, a substitute for it, and is therefore a sign in a special sense. The fugitive identification of the sign as 'ideological body' (*FM*, 126) manages to convey that combined concrete and figurative sense in a single (somewhat infelicitous) formulation. It also supports Bakhtin's view that 'Language in the novel not only represents, but itself serves as the object of representation' (*DI*, 49). According to this conception of the word-sign, in its unique, aesthetic manifestation, both signifier and signified are united within the word, as a self-referential sign.

In another context yielding the same result, where 'theme' refers to signified and 'form' to signifier, the point is again affirmed in *Marxism and the Philosophy of Language*, when it is stated that 'The theme of an ideological sign and the form of an ideological sign are inextricably bound together and are separable only in the abstract' (22). Either formulation, Bakhtin's or Voloshinov's more semiotically-oriented terminology, clearly does away with the prospect of any lingering specter of a form/content dichotomy, assigning the artistic sign a special role in the process.

Thus, in narrative, where authorial intent (of some kind) is presumed to exist, the word is viewed both as materially present and as image representing the character or his creator (in some narratorial guise) as ideological construct or bearer of an idea. In noting the artistic sign's specialized quality, Bakhtin observes with regard to the genre he came to favor: 'The image of another's language and outlook on the world, simultaneously represented *and* representing, is extremely typical of the novel . . . [All] essentially novelistic images share this quality: they are internally dialogized images – of the languages, styles, world views of another . . .' (*DI*, 45, 46). The motivating ideas, governing thoughts, and entire structure of the mind of the fictional character are thus exteriorized and depicted through the image created by language. More-over, that image need not be pictorial (or aural) but ideo-logical, conveying a character's quality of mind through the novelist's choice of identifying words, whose internal complexities and structure represent a composite sign of that mind.

Bakhtin is concerned to demonstrate that discourse in narrative is structured as '*verbal* artistic representation' (*DI*, 332). The word in the novel serves to create an image – or, better, is itself that image – of what it purports to represent. This kind of structure is both ideological and semiological. To separate the two aspects amounts to a contradiction in terms. Since the sign is by nature ideologi-cal, the word as sign is necessarily imbued with that same inherent quality. Hence 'The domain of ideology coincides with the domain of signs. They equate with one another. Wherever a sign is present ideology is present, too. *Every-thing ideological possesses semiotic value. . . . The word is the ideological phenomenon par excellence'* (*MPL*, 10, 13). In such unequivocal *semiotic* terms is the entire matter formulated.[1]

Following (in this one respect) the Swiss linguist Ferdinand de Saussure, the word as sign is deemed both arbitrary and conventional in this line of thought (*FM*, 120). Although potentially embracing a wide range of possible signification, when 'confined' to the dictionary the word remains essentially devoid of meaning. It can only be realized within its concrete historical utilization – that is, when employed at a certain time within a particular context. The greater its usage, affording a corresponding distinctly varied accentuation, the greater its vitality. Hence the animating claim that 'It is precisely a word's multiaccentuality that makes it a living thing' (*MPL*, 81). Only through its concrete usage, we may conclude, does the word acquire its special meaning or 'theme'.[2]

As a result of its concrete contextual usage, the word is wrung free from its potentially rich and abundant set of generalized meanings – in the dual sense of having a particular significance attached to it by the sender and of being apprehended in some fashion (ideally, corresponding to the manner intended) by the receiver. In Saussurian terms, the word is divested of its possible broad inclusive meaning as part of *langue* (or range of grammatical possibility, rejected by Bakhtin as a purely abstract, insubstantial category), and is realized as a concrete, individualized utterance, from Bakhtin's perspective, a word's only possible meaningful manifestation. From an abstract situation characterized by arbitrariness, conventionality, and wide range of possible utilization, the word acquires meaning by virtue of its specific implementation and concurrent reception.[3]

It is precisely that specificity, moreover, that affords the potential for the word to function in its truest role as dialogical entity. 'Any utterance – the finished, written utterance not excepted – makes response to something and is calculated to be responded to in turn' (*MPL*, 72). In terms of the internal dynamics that informs the word with its heralded dialogical nature, however, the word acquires its individualized meaning in a given context either primarily from the addresser or from the addressee (but not exclusively from either), depending largely upon the perspective of the one in relation to the other and to the word itself (its particular accentuation, identified by Bakhtin as its 'intonation'). The idea is expressed thus: '*any locution actually said aloud or written down for intelligible communication* (that is, anything but words merely reposing in a dictionary) *is the expression and product of the social interaction of three participants*: the *speaker* (author), *the listener* (reader), and *the topic* (the who or what) *of speech . . .*' (*Discourse*, 105). On some rudimentary level, however, it is necessary to come to grips with the dynamics that this notion entails.

To this end, Bakhtin emphasizes the importance of the addresser and his use of the word as follows; '*Who* speaks and under what conditions he speaks: this is what determines the word's actual meaning' (*DI*, 401). The dialogical nature of the word therefore emanates in large part from the choice of a particular utterance on the part of the addresser, who inevitably takes into consideration the status and relationship of the addressee. The former, in effect, chooses his words 'with a sideward glance' at the latter. The word is thus seen as a '*two-sided* act. It is determined both by *whose* word it is and for *whom* it is meant. As word, it is precisely *the product of the reciprocal relationship between speaker and listener, addresser and addressee*'. It makes a difference on the most fundamental level, in other words, whom one addresses, since the word exists within a given utterance as the result of a dependent considered choice. 'Each and every word expresses the "one" in relation to the "other". . . . A word is territory shared by both addresser and addressee, by the speaker and his interlocutor' (*MPL*, 86).

Moreover, since the word is conceived as requisite to every instance of understanding and effort at interpretation, it is possessed of an unqualified 'social ubiquity' that may be conceived as follows. 'The immediate social situation and the broader social milieu wholly determine – and determine within, so to speak – the structure of an utterance' (*MPL*, 15, 19, 86). Here 'the immediate social situation' may be understood as the particular relationship between addresser and addressee just noted; while 'the broader social milieu' refers to that aspect of the word which bonds it to a certain segment of the population, particular time period, or other cultural determinant. Its locus of meaning is thus determined by a certain immediacy coupled with a broad generality.

From these linked perspectives, the word is conceived as a complex mosaic of ever-shifting nuances, connotations, and meanings. At the same time it is thoroughly penetrated with the intersecting ideological 'accents' of earlier intentions. The word is thus an unstable structure, whose locus of concrete meaning or 'theme' is dependent upon the associations and bonds attributed to it by society as a whole, and by the accentuation afforded it within concrete instances of its previous usage. Its meaning and sense continually shift as a result of certain accents diminishing in frequency and intensity, while others are concomitantly augmented and changed. Hence, the word itself belongs to no one and to everyone; no one can claim it as his own, since it is permeated already with the past intentions of the other. Yet, as a matter of virtual due course, inherent within each unique application, there remains for each user the opportunity to make a creative contribution of one's own.

CHRONOTOPE

Distinct, structurally motivated concepts of time and space in the literary work are both indispensable and inseparable. As the fundamental instance of discourse, the word as sign may be conceived as situated at the intersection of two interconnected planes: the temporal and spatial. A unifying ideal concept or model, Bakhtin's idea of the 'chronotope' specifies the 'intrinsic connectedness of temporal and spatial relationships that are artistically expressed in literature' (*DI*, 84). As the source of genre-specific thematic material, the chronotope, in abstract formulation, permits the artistic realization of an

event in time and space. 'All the novel's astract elements –
philosophical and social generalizations, ideas, analyses of
cause and effect – gravitate toward the chronotope and
through it take on flesh and blood, permitting the imaging
power of art to do its work' (*DI*, 250). Conversely, without
the presence of the chronotope, which situates the artistic
image, there would remain only a lifeless abstraction existing beyond the limits of novelistic conception. The chronotope thus specifies the time/space coordinates of 'any and
every literary image' (*DI*, 251), conveying to the reader the
social and historical dimensions of texts.

In the broadest sense, the chronotope is constituted by
cultural time and space, meaning that cultural codes in
conjunction with generic norms are its principal determi-
nants. Likewise, the internal form of the word itself is
significantly chronotopic. Thus when Bakhtin declares

> Discourse lives, as it were, on the boundary between its
> own context and another, alien, context (*DI*, 284)

he is affirming the word's temporal orientation, since each
context is necessarily a *successive* context. As one speaker
yields to another, the word acquires meaning at the juncture of its necessarily different usage by each. When
Bakhtin states

> As a living, socio-ideological concrete thing, as hetero-
> glot opinion, language, for the individual conscious-
> ness, lies on the borderline between oneself and the
> other (*DI*, 293)

he is declaring the word's spatial orientation in terms of its
users, whereby the spatial plane is viewed as implying a
certain interhuman, communicative space. In addition,
when it is affirmed

> Discourse lives, as it were, beyond itself, in a living
> impulse toward the object . . . (*DI*, 292)

the word's spatial orientation with respect to its specific

referent in a given context is acknowledged. In this equally important sense, the spatial plane is defined to include the object to which the word refers in all of its varied accentual transformations. The spatial plane thus retains a certain dual aspect, incorporating both the object (in its myriad conceptions and depictions) and the user, as speaker and listener (in all of his or her multitudinous temporal manifestations).

In Bakhtin's view, as noted, there is no such thing as 'the word as such' – except as it exists in the dictionary; as a 'living thing', the word is always contextual. Moreover, 'the word does not enter the utterance from a dictionary, but from life, from utterance to utterance' (*FM*, 122). Beyond a word's 'neutral signification' or dictionary definition, it bears an 'actual meaning' (*DI*, 281), which essentially corresponds to the intention of the addresser at each individual utterance – none of which will entirely coincide. The lack of a distinction made between the living, dialogic word and its lifeless counterpart represents for Bakhtin the chief failure of linguistics and the philosophy of language. By contrast, according to his proposed study, every word is by definition permeated with the past meanings and intentions of others – with inhering specific contextual, emotional, historical, or biographical overtones, which are immanent in the word prior to the speaker's usage, itself implying at least in part a new set of intentions appropriate to the particular context at hand.

The dynamics of discourse affirmed by Bakhtin's dialogics may be expressed in the following triadic relation. The word is uttered by a single individual at a given moment; it owes its 'composition' – its nuances, connotations, and the meanings already adhering to it – to previous usage by numerous other individuals; at the same time it is directed toward the as yet unuttered responsive word of still others. In terms of its temporal features, the word in its concrete present form is oriented both toward the past, because of the numerous meanings and connotations associated with it, and toward the future, as a reply anticipating some further response. The word is articulated in material form in the present, has been largely 'composed' in the past, and is further determined by its future 'expectations'– that it will be accepted or rejected, be turned ironically back upon itself, will open up additional possibilities for discussion or foreclose on others. The word exists at the intersection of all past and present intentions with which it is permeated, and will, ideally, prove adequate to confront a possible future response as well. It bears a past-oriented 'regressive relevance' conjoined to a future-oriented 'progressive significance', but is itself articulated in a dynamic present replete with the potential for further verbal interaction or dialogical confrontation. As Bakhtin declares: 'Understanding and response are dialectically merged and mutually condition each other; one is impossible without the other' (*DI*, 282). Here 'understanding' implies a comprehension of past usages of the word, while 'response' has to do with the future, with the word's as yet unutilized potential within a current or new context. Bearing a past orientation as an inherent, immutable part of its present meaning and intention, the word incorporates a concurrent future orientation as well: 'every word is directed toward an *answer* and cannot escape the profound influence of the answering word that it anticipates' (*DI*, 280).[4] The word in its temporal aspect thus appears as a 'dual-directed sign' that takes cognizance of past usages by others, but whose present intentions are simultaneously focused upon the potential future response of a current interlocutor engaged in dialogue.

In sum, the internally dialogized word is both multifaceted and multidirected, existing at the confluence of two planes. Articulated in the present, it is oriented toward both past and future as joint temporal considerations. In spatial terms, it refers to the object (itself permeated by past and future intentions), to previous users of the word (in some necessarily differing sets of contexts), and to those who have yet to employ it (in some as yet undefined context). Yet through all such complex temporal and spatial orientation and interpenetration, through both realized and potential interaction, the word remains – in each individual concrete utterance – *unique*, since the specific situation of its singular usage is ultimately unrepeatable, while the nuances adhering to it are augmented and enriched by its 'present' employment.

In his efforts to effect *'a sharpened dialogic relationship to the word'* (*DI*, 352), Bakhtin thus seeks to reconcile the word's material presence with its being the concrete manifestation of an image designed to convey an ideological position; he attempts to show it as existing at the critical juncture where an event in time is materialized in space; and to illustrate its interrelated facets of being both ideological and social, and therefore semiological. But most important is his concept that the word is by nature dialogical, and thus inherently bears a seemingly unlimited ability to generate dialogue as the considered response to another's (or one's own) already articulated or as yet unuttered word.

3

The Novel

The novel is a different breed, and with it and in it is
born the future of all literature.

Bakhtin, 'Epic and Novel'

'Expansion. That is the idea the novelist must cling to. Not
completion. Not rounding off but opening out.' Asserted
by E.M. Forster in his 1927 book, *Aspects of the Novel*, that
injunction captures the spirit informing Bakhtin's view of
the novel. But for their prescriptive aspect and tone,
Forster's words might appear to belong to the Russian
literary theoretician. Whereas, in his treatise, the English
novelist and critic quickly moved on to other considerations of his subject, Bakhtin made the point of 'Not
rounding off but opening out' the central feature of his
own discussion of the novel. In Bakhtin's thought the
novel is given preeminence as the quintessential register
of society's attitudes toward itself and the world. That
quality allows for the novel to serve as contemporary
vehicle for philosophical investigation. 'When the novel
becomes the dominant genre', writes Bakhtin, 'epistem-
ology becomes the dominant discipline' (*DI*, 15). Further,
as the genre opposed to all others in its efforts to counteract common rigidifying tendencies in literature, the novel
bears the potential to incorporate other more clearly delineated genres within itself, and thus appears inherently to
expand its own chimerical confines, while at the same
time resisting definition.

In an attempt at least partially to overcome that resistance, the term 'novel' will be employed here in three
interrelated ways: in the broad generic sense of whatever
we mean when we refer to the Novel as such; in the vastly
reduced sense of any individual work representative,

simply, of the genre; and, finally, in the sense of the 'novel', or a distinctive complex of its distinguishing features, serving as model for the making of novels. Derived essentially from Bakhtin's thought, but an extension of it as well, this last concern, in particular, bears directly on the possibility of establishing a broadly applicable poetics, or theory, of the novel. Bakhtin's concept of the chronotope points in this direction, since this time/space model is itself designed to elaborate the generative mechanisms by which narratives exhibiting common structural features are produced in a particular place at a certain historical moment.

Bakhtin's views on the novel do not constitute a cohesive theory or system, nor, according to his argument, could there be one. His essays on the novel represent instead a thoroughly innovative and engaging series of chapters on the history and development of the novel. Aspects of those 'chapters' may be appropriated to advance related efforts to elaborate a poetics of the novel in general or one of its main lines in particular. From Bakhtin's viewpoint, however, the formulation of a theory of the novel would entail its constant revision and reformulation by virtue of its inherently fluid subject matter. Since the novel itself is in a state of constant flux and dynamic change, no final all-encompassing theory could ever be elaborated – unless the novel form itself would someday ultimately rigidify into a static, forever stratified system of its own. Barring that unlikely eventuality, all theories of the novel would themselves remain *developing* theories, encompassing their subject to greater or lesser degree in an ongoing process of complementary artistic and philosophic creativity.

Bakhtin regards the novel as 'the sole genre that continues to develop, that is as yet uncompleted'. In declaring the novel 'the genre of becoming' (*DI*, 3, 22), Bakhtin is in accord with Georg Lukács, who similarly affirms that 'the novel, in contrast to other genres whose existence resides within the finished form, appears as something in process of becoming' (1971:72–3). Both thinkers view the epic, in contradistinction to the novel, as the quintessential completed form. However, while the Hungarian Marxist critic looks back with a certain nostalgia to the ancient originating form, the Russian theorist looks with approbation upon its later, modern manifestation. For Bakhtin, moreover, in a seemingly injudicious assessment, virtually all other genres have similarly completed their development. Individual representative works within them only further support and sustain the canon by which they themselves were conceived and formed. Texts other than the novel legitimate the genre by which they are defined and which they in turn define by virtue of their existence within it. But the novel, by contrast, has no established canon or norm by which its representative instances are created. It exists as an open-ended series of related but individual texts which further extend the genre's ever-expanding 'boundaries'. The novel is thus the individualized text par excellence, whose interconnections with other such texts may be tenuous, since no definitive set of norms may be said to apply. Yet each novel reinvigorates and revitalizes the generic concept of the Novel by its very existence as a *sui generis* product within a heterogeneous series of related but frequently very different set of forms.

How are they related, we need ask, if not according to some predetermined or clearly delimited canon? One way to approach – or, perhaps, detour – the problem is to take recourse in such engaging existential formulations as those proposed by Lukács: 'The novel is the epic of a world that has been abandoned by God'. It is that form 'whose very matter is seeking and failing to find the essence' (1971:88, 122). But such 'existential' assessments clearly do not delineate the novel's constitutive elements, nor do they afford any real possibility for elaborating a poetics of the novel. On a different tack, it may be noted that most works termed novels nonetheless share certain common features, or are at least recognized as such, since readers share a common conception of what it means to refer to a work of verbal art as a novel. What this shared conception entails is perhaps the relatively extended length of the work, its being composed of integrated mimetic and diegetic discourse, the presence of characters whose life stories or portions thereof are presented constituting a distinguishable plot, the recognition that the interplay of time and space considerations are crucial factors within that plot, and that their presentation from a certain perspective or point of view is also critical. Yet these and other related general features do not define the novel, since they are not exclusive to it but pertain as well in some degree to other narrative forms. Hence the novel's resistance to definition is quickly demonstrated.

Considered broadly from Bakhtin's perspective, the concept of genre is conceived as 'a zone and a field of valorized perception . . . a mode for representing the world' (*DI*, 28). Unmistakable in its lineaments, such a view is clearly drawn from the veritable tradition that conceives of art as mimesis, as a vast, intricately related modeling system of the world. Thus, the elaborate temporal and spatial configurations that govern the perception of the actual world (from the standpoint of a given culturally engrained perspective) are those that determine as well the making of a text. As Bakhtin puts it: 'Out of the chronotopes of our world (which serve as the source of representation) emerge the reflected and *created* chronotopes of the world represented in the work . . .' (*DI*, 253). Or, otherwise expressed: 'Since authors model whole worlds, they are ineluctably forced to employ the organizing categories of the worlds that they themselves inhabit' (Clark and Holquist 1984:278). But the process also works in reverse, as both the world and the world of the text appropriate what they need from one another, in the fundamental human activity of making sense of the world through art, resulting in a series of potentially infinite progressions. 'However forcefully the real and the represented world resist fusion . . . they are nevertheless indissolubly tied up with each other and find themselves in continual mutual interaction. . . . The work and the world represented in it enter the real world and enrich it, and the real world enters the work and its world as part of the process of its creation . . .' (*DI*, 254). In result, this mutually influenced, dual-directed flow of information – from which the novel is derived – may be directly attri-

buted to the merging of the cultural codes of the actual
world with the literary codes governing the represented
world of the novel. For it is the concatenation of these two
distinctly related normative systems that affords this literary form its modeling capability in the first place.[1]

From a related point of departure, the concept of genre
may be conceived in terms of three gradations. The first is
exemplified by the epic, which is antiquated and no longer
engenders further production. Second are those still vital
genres which merit such designation as abstract literary
forms within whose bounds additional representative
works continue to be generated, and where the latter,
conversely, are defined by those bounds or specific canon.
Finally, there is the novel, itself essentially undefined,
representative instances of which repeatedly and insistently extend its generic 'bounds', so that the metaphoric
term specifying its non-existent boundaries is ultimately
devalued: the novel knows no bounds. Of consequence,
then, for the moment, is the recognition simply that the
novel is a form opposed to all other genres, which have
either ceased to generate further texts (as in the case of the
epic), or which only engender additional representative
instances strictly within the given canon. By contrast, in
the absence of a clearly defined set of norms, the Novel
emerges as a self-revivifying genre through the proliferation of new individualized texts that further extend its
sphere.

In heralding the novel as a breed apart, Bakhtin notes
those features that distinguish it from other genres. First
among these is his concept of 'polyphony', applied originally to the Dostoevsky novel, as a more specialized
formulation of his broadly conceived principle of dialogism. Just as the American philosopher C.S. Peirce regarded the process of semiosis – the exchange of signs and
their concomitant interpretation – as a potentially endless
human activity, so did Bakhtin conceive of human communication in analogous terms. It is therefore not surpris-
ing that he consistently privileges 'unfinishedness' over
completion, openness over closure, and a 'centrifugal' as
opposed to a 'centripetal' orientation, where the latter

attempts to make things cohere through a reductivist tendency, while the former is informed by a confirmed openness to the world and the possibility of further dialogical engagement. Centrifugal forces, for Bakhtin, thus seek 'to keep the world open to becoming' (Clark and Holquist 1984:80) in opposition to the centripetal impulse that strives to effect a corresponding closure on the text. Realized generally as the Novel, but concretely as one of a potentially infinite series of possible manifestations, such formalized text owes its existence and may trace its historical development to 'the current of decentralizing, centrifugal forces' (*DI*, 273). Yet the multiform use of language in the actual world and in the world of the novel nevertheless exhibits fundamental qualities of both a centrifugal and centripetal nature. Both forces exist in the utterance, articulated either in everyday speech as perhaps some brief, ill-considered response or in the world of verbal art as a carefully formulated, extensive work. The one force opens the text with an outward thrust, the other shuts it down by counteracting the possibility for further dialogical response. Hence, the dialectics of language use, on whatever plane, precludes the generalized manifestation of the one tendency without the presence of the other. However, at any given moment, one will be clearly seen to predominate in their ubiquitous contrapuntal juxtaposition. In the case of the novel, the centrifugal is valorized by Bakhtin as the more dynamic, generally dominant tendency, generating at numerous felicitous 'moments' new forms as further potential models for extending the boundaries of a genre which is inherently boundless.

Underlying this broadly applicable concept of contrapuntal juxtaposition, where the one generative force counteracts successfully the delimiting tendency of the other, is Bakhtin's all-encompassing, dominant theme of dialogic relations, which, as the governing principle of his thought, is conceived to exist among all elements of novelistic structure. Yet the clearly evident juxtapositions among them may not always appear explicit. As an analogous case in point, Bakhtin's discussion of the 'internally persuasive word', as he terms it, is both relevant and instructive. Implicitly juxtaposed in a given text to the 'authoritative word', which seeks to foreclose on possible further dialogue by virtue of its presupposed capacity for finalization, the internally persuasive word, with its attendant emphasis on affording new perspectives and related modes of conceptualization, is seen as a fundamental source of the novel form existing in embryo. 'The semantic structure of an internally persuasive discourse is *not finite*, it is *open*; in each of the new contexts that dialogize it, this discourse is able to reveal ever newer *ways to mean*' (*DI*, 346). In distinguishing the novel form from among other genres, Bakhtin might well have said essentially the same thing in this related but very much expanded context.

Bakhtin's rejection of finishedness represents a crucial aspect of his thought, but the *possibility* of completion is of complementary importance as the source of a vital and necessary tension. This may be illustrated in the opposition between what is 'given' (*dan*) or established, in his terminology, and what is 'conceived' (*zadan*) or posited, and is therefore still in progress. That opposition distinguishes between something already finished and forever closed to further creative (or dialogical) endeavor as opposed to there yet remaining (perhaps forever) a ready potential for creating a certain 'completedness' – but one which is not to be achieved so long as there is life and the possibility of extended dialogue, yielding greater differentiation and change. Thus, the (never-ending) project of conceiving and, consequently, of attempting to complete the self, for instance, is an ongoing life-affirming process. One works toward the formation (or formulation) of a self, an understanding of the other, the comprehension of a text. Yet the completion of these interrelated tasks is both unrealizable and ultimately unwanted. Rather, what is sought and valued, on numerous planes of both quotidian discourse and cultural endeavor, is a multiplicity of communicative utterances, evidenced among individuals engaged in dialogue as its most proliferated manifestation. Hence the articulation of an utterance, the making of a self, striving to understand the other or to comprehend a text are all creative acts.

TEMPORAL UNIFORMITY

Also singled out by Bakhtin as distinctive to the novel and requisite to its continued thriving as a 'genre of becoming' are its 'maximal contact with the present' and its 'multi-languaged consciousness' (*DI*, 11), distinguishing the novel in both respects from all preceding genres. Chief among these, for contrastive purposes, the epic serves Bakhtin (and Lukács) as the principal pole of diametric opposition to the novel in several areas of related concern. First, the fundamental dichotomy of 'closed' and 'open' applies to the epic and novel, respectively, where the former is the product of a completed, 'monologic' perspective on the world and is 'finished, conclusive, and immutable' (*DI*, 17), while the latter bears a dialogical orientation that is 'contested, contestable and contesting' (*DI*, 332), and, as a result, is forever unfinished – as genre and as individual text. The one literary form is thus not 'given' but 'conceived', as it awaits the completing act of the reader. But this in itself comprises a paradoxical situation, since such finalizing effort is by definition individualistic, historically and culturally determined, and therefore essentially peripheral and ephemeral. Truth and meaning, in other words, belong to no one at any given moment but exist rather as a potentially emergent feature of dialogical engagement.

Whereas the epic presents a valorized absolute past, which is self-enclosed and self-reflexive, with no orientation toward some future development, the novel is centered in the present, itself conceived as a temporal model characterized by its developing, evolutionary nature, its spontaneity, incompleteness and inconclusiveness, by its ability and commitment to rethink and reevaluate. 'The present is something transitory, it is flow, it is an eternal continuation without beginning or end; it is denied an authentic conclusiveness and consequently lacks an essence as well' (*DI*, 20). In such seemingly negative formulation does Bakhtin in turn valorize the novel's present as an epistemological and axiological pivot, affording its truth-seeking hero the opportunity to learn, experiment, test his powers, and perhaps fail – all of which is inconceivable in the epic, where everything is 'given' and known as a set of values from that period in time when time had stopped, or, better, when it had not yet begun to move. When a work is centered in the present, however, 'The temporal model of the world changes radically: it becomes a world where there is no first word (no ideal word), and the final word has not yet been spoken' (*DI*, 30). Yet it is a model that affords as well the possibility of 'an authentically objective portrayal of the past as the past' (*DI*, 29), since it is a past that ultimately acknowledges and allows for the present. And by the same simple logic, the present, of course, moves toward the future, eventually allowing for that open-ended segment also to become present. The novel's 'temporal model of the world' – its present – is thus able to recapture a past which bears a relation to the present, rather than only to itself, and which is at the same time future-directed, and therefore unresolved and inconclusive.[2] Yet it is this very indeterminateness that affords the potential for 'an eternal re-thinking and re-evaluating' (*DI*, 31) that distinguishes the novel from the epic in the first place. Expressed in different but complementary terms, the one is monologic in its ideological orientation and manner of expression, the other is dialogic.

LINGUISTIC DIVERSITY

A constitutive factor by which monologic tendencies are counteracted in the novel is appropriated under the term 'heteroglossia', designating two related concepts (conveyed by the two closely derived Bakhtinian expressions: *raznorečie* and *raznorečivost'*). Appropriately termed Bakhtin's 'master trope' for elucidating his theory of the novel (*DI*, xix; ed.), heteroglossia is designed, first, to convey the sense of a creative tension originating from the constant struggle between centripetal and centrifugal forces, evidenced in the generalized context of the novel by the opposition between a conceivably dominant literary language and mutually contending extraliterary languages that are striving to move from the realm of everyday oral discourse to that of literature. The struggle between the one centralizing impulse and other decentralizing tendencies is thus underscored by the term, which succinctly points to the problem of intra-language stratification or internal differentiation as one that nevertheless inherently bears the seeds for its felicitous resolution in verbal art. Such linguistic contention, in other words, affords the possibility for dynamic interaction rather than static stabilization, where the former implies the need to intermesh the unifying, centripetal aspects of the literary language that identify a work as conforming to the current (but fluid) constraints of the novel form with those differentiating, centrifugal features that seek neither conformity nor uniformity within the canon but singular individualized expression instead. Yet at the same time this new resultant hypothetical construct must also be construed – appropriately (given the etymology of the word) – as a novel.

Second, heteroglossia designates the presence in the novel of languages that are socio-ideological: those belonging to certain professions, genres, or particular generations, affording a multiplicity of diverse levels of speech used in daily discourse but transposed to the novel. This linguistic stratification thus corresponds on the fundamental level of language, as the raw material from which verbal art is made, to Bakhtin's notion of the genre itself as a self-critical, differentiative, and ever-expanding form. As linguistic usage further stratifies and proliferates in various spheres and directions, so does the novel, which inevitably follows suit. This tendency of the novel to tread the cutting edge of two opposing orientations results in an intentional linguistic diversity characteristic of what Clark and Holquist term (by analogy to Bakhtin's broadly encompassing expression) the 'heteroglot' as distinct from the 'monoglot' novel (1984:291–3). In the latter form all of the characters are attributed a uniform manner of speech, while in the former a clear distinction is made between speech patterns characteristic of various social strata and other distinguishing features. In this manner the fictional world is rendered diverse rather than uniform, since the affinity of the actual world for proliferating new and rarefied forms of linguistic expression is thereby acknowledged within the novel's heteroglottic linguistic plane. As Bakhtin affirms: 'The language of the novel is a *system* of languages that mutually and ideologically interanimate each other. . . . It is a system of intersecting planes' (*DI*, 47, 48). This single affirmation affords a profuse set of related ramifications. First, such system of 'intersecting planes' derives in part from the fact that individuals in the actual world as well as characters in the fictional draw upon the general linguistic pool for their respective means of expression, but one which is nevertheless conjoined and informed by their own highly individualized use of language. Expressed crudely, but conforming to Bakhtin's general argument, everyone has his own 'language'. This fact is fully capitalized upon in the novel, where a character is created, first of all, to speak, and whose utterances are designed on some level to express a certain ideology. But that ideology is formulated in profoundly complex manner, whereby utterances are derived from an intentional diversity of speech [*raznorečivost'*], which may be transformed into diversity of language [*raznojazyčie*], ultimately resulting in 'a dialogue of languages' (*DI*, 294).

Conversely, if each speaker, as Bakhtin holds, employs language distinctively and, perhaps, idiosyncratically, then each is certain to speak 'a different language'. This implies the need to translate. Communication thus always involves translation. In the special case of the novel, however, where the character expresses himself in some 'heteroglot' fashion, he is bound, from Bakhtin's perspective, to emerge as an ideologue to some degree, by virtue of his individualized lexicon and particular manner of expression. These latter interrelated facets are in turn construed as a series of 'ideologemes' which, of necessity, express a specific point of view on the world. Further, as forms for conceptualizing the world, such given views, interrelated with others – both explicitly within the novel's established confines and, perhaps, implicitly beyond them

– make of the novel, in Bakhtin's phrase, 'a dialogical representation of an ideologically freighted discourse . . .' (*DI*, 333). In other words, every word articulated in the novel is by definition both social and ideological, collectively replicating an arena accommodating various contending points of view. While that novelistic word is projected as being, first, the word of 'a speaking human being', Bakhtin claims as well that 'Characteristic for the novel as a genre is not the image of a man in his own right, but a man who is precisely the *image of a language*'. In this respect, as Bakhtin argues further, 'The central problem for a stylistics of the novel may be formulated as the problem of *artistically representing language, the problem of representing the image of a language*' (*DI*, 336). The novelist must therefore create, as the bearer of a certain set of ideologemes, not only a believable speaking figure, but one whose utterances and choice of language reflect back upon or, better, clearly coincide with that figure as signs adequately representing the character's expressed ideology. That is, the character must be 'pictured' *in* and *by* his words, producing his image in language, to the extent that such endeavor might be effectively realized. By these lights, the character is defined precisely by what he says – which is in accord, given the initial premises of Bakhtin's argument, with why he was created in the first place.

Finally, from the perspective of a relatively non-traditional centrifugal force endeavoring in an inherent struggle with a more conservative centripetal orientation to keep language 'alive and developing', the internal dynamics of the novel – as opposed to all other genres – are seen by Bakhtin to conform most closely with the dynamics operative in natural language, where, 'alongside verbal–ideological centralization and unification, the uninterrupted processes of decentralization and disunification go forward' (*DI*, 272). For Bakhtin, the language of the novel is similarly stratified according to a system of 'languages' that are socio-ideological. The result is, as he terms it, 'dialogized heteroglossia', which represents the confluence of two or more ideological points of view potentially at work within a single utterance. Every novel, to some extended degree, then, exhibits this defining characteristic, which sets it apart from other genres, but which also brings it closer to the posited workings of natural language, upon which all genres must naturally draw.

THE NOVEL AS MODEL

Bakhtin observes that at those times in history when the novel form tends to predominate it also serves to 'novelize' other genres. It accomplishes this by liberating them 'from all that serves as a brake on their unique development' and by 'inserting' into those other genres 'an indeterminacy, a certain semantic openendedness, a living contact with unfinished, still-evolving contemporary reality (the open-ended present)' (*DI*, 39, 7). The same might be said of the novel's novelization of the Novel – that is, when a single work revitalizes and extends the genre's non-existent 'bounds'. Thus Bakhtin writes that the 'great heroes' of literature and language 'turn out to be first and foremost genres' (*DI*, 8). But within what Bakhtin himself regards as the special case of the novel, which has no canon of its own, one must seek the 'hero' of this paradoxical genre in the models (such as the chronotope) from which the various constitutive modes or forms of the novel derive. For in endeavoring to do so, the novel's crucial role as social document, as Bakhtin conceives of it, is further enhanced through the recognition of certain codes and values of a given time and place being reflected in the work – as either promoted or rejected in the world – in an ongoing socio-historical process forever destined to change. Specific chronotopic features are therefore presumed inherent within the novel at a particular historical moment, making it distinctive and defining it as such.

When Bakhtin observes that 'the novel has no canon of its own', and when he notes the 'ability of the novel to criticize itself' (*DI*, 3, 6), he comes near to acknowledging that the concept of the 'novel' as a certain culturally and historically defined ideological configuration may serve as a model (or aggregate of characteristic elements) for the Novel. A set of constitutive features is to be conceived, in other words, as being particular to the novel at any given point in its historical development. Derived from the cultural codes of the times, its general features would include (among others) social, linguistic, sartorial and behavioral concerns; in short, those particular distinguishing aspects which are a part of the 'novel' *as model* at some period in its development. For additional, more specific instances, we might draw upon nineteenth-century Russian literature, for example, which documents such cultural detail as the gathering of the upper class in salons, the usage of French in those salons as the primary means of communication, the fighting of duels within that same class for the sake of honor (as a similarly codified, alternative means of 'communication'); the indication of class distinctions through certain forms of address ('Your Honor!') or specialized language (the added, hyphenated 's' in Russian to indicate obeisance ['Sir!'] toward a social superior); a peasant's mode of dress in contrast to an urban dweller's; a lackey's mode of conduct as opposed to his master's; and so forth. Such thematic and linguistic elements (the list could be extended indefinitely) constitute the components of the 'novel' understood as model for the Novel at a certain synchronic episode in its history. But these elements are not necessarily a part of the novel's – also ever-changing – *generic* aspects. Hence the distinction made here is between the Novel as a genre of a special sort, as Bakhtin would have it, and the 'novel' as model for the making of further individualized texts referred to as 'novels' because they are either designed or expected to bring something new to the realm of verbal art.

This view, as extension of Bakhtin's thought, acknowledges the possibility of formulating a generally applicable poetics of the Novel – but with a certain proviso. If one accepts the criterial characteristics of an undisputed open-endedness and orientation toward what Bakhtin terms a 'centrifugal' mode of development as being not necessarily salutary but simply typical and explanatory of the

genre's vitality, then one must also acknowledge that to
establish a viable poetics would entail a necessarily repeated *re*formulation and extension of that poetics analogous to and accommodating of the genre encompassed
within its purview. A self-generating and self-renewing
genre, in other words, requires a like poetics: one that is
geared toward its further (ongoing) elaboration but which
may also be delimited according to specific chronotopic
features, as Bakhtin has shown. This supposition allows,
first of all, for the possibility of establishing interpretive
models, designed to accommodate a given instance of the
novel, and affording as well the possibility for a certain
creative potential in the hands of the gifted critic. In
addition, any such interpretive model, employed concretely as part of a specific critical endeavor, or as ideal
construct assailing a poetics of the novel (in abstract theoretical terms), would necessarily acknowledge a similarly
ever-changing use of language as the material basis of
verbal art in general and of the Novel as its perhaps most
variegated 'breed'.

The two linked concepts of the Novel as genre and the
'novel' as model, it should be underscored in conclusion,
must be conceived as interlocked and interdependent,
rather than juxtaposed. For, on the one hand, the novel
continually redefines itself on the basis of what its makers
and readers at a given time conceive it to be. But, on the
other, as a series of forever varying and contrastive constitutive elements, this latter consideration – the problem of
what the novel is conceived to be at any given moment – is
at the same time regarded by both the novelist and reader/
critic alike as the *model* by which the novel is created by the
one and read and evaluated by the other.

4
Self and Other

Art and life are not one, but should become one in me, in the unity of my responsibility.

Bakhtin, 'Art and Responsibility'

The distinction between the self and other is fundamental to Bakhtin's thinking as philosopher of language and literary theorist. Even more so, perhaps, it is central to what can only be termed a profound spiritual message. Thus, while astutely commenting on the art of Dostoevsky, Bakhtin theorizes on the art of living.

I am conscious of myself and become myself only while revealing myself for another, through another, and with the help of another. The most important acts constituting self-consciousness are determined by a relationship toward another consciousness (toward a *thou*). . . . The very being of man (both external and internal) is the *deepest communion. To be* means *to communicate.* . . . To be means to be for another, and through the other, for oneself. A person has no internal sovereign territory, he is wholly and always on the boundary: looking inside himself, he looks *into the eyes of another* or *with the eyes of another.* . . . I cannot manage without another, I cannot become myself without another; I must find myself in another by finding another in myself (in mutual reflection and mutual acceptance). (*PDP*, 287)

In the mutually reflective realms of life and art, and in the linked concepts of individuals and their individual use of language, the sense of the other in relation to the self is accorded striking affirmation as a formative influence. As the requisite to dialogical interaction in the territory of art as well as life, the other assists in the ongoing process of determining the self, which also means determining the word of the self. Basic to the formulation of one's own utterance in discourse is the other's word or utterance. For the other may be conceived as an individual characterized by a distinctive use of language that contributes to make the self individual and distinct from all others in *his* use of language. In a perhaps even more crucial respect, the other is formative of the self in the sense that one is not able to know oneself without the interacting presence of the other.

Bakhtin approaches the problem of the self and other primarily in terms of one's 'own' speech and the 'alien' word of the other. Yet the term 'alien' (*čužoj*) is curiously deceptive. Each self is alien, first of all, only in the sense of being 'other' to all other individuals. A principal feature of one's otherness derives from the particular application and use of language by the self from among all possibilities. The choice of one's language to express a point of view is indeed as distinctive as a set of fingerprints or signature. One's distinctive use of language is thus a critical sign of oneself. It is what makes one other to all others and an individual to the self. But the word of the self also expresses a world view; each message bears that view as an encapsulated ideology. One creates oneself through one's own use of language – but so is the other's language formative of the self, since an utterance is formulated only in the light of another's speech.

The speaking subject in both literature and life formulates his utterance as a message directed at a particular receiver. Every message exists within a context which consists of utterances made by both interlocutors. No word is articulated in a vacuum devoid of context. Such context consists, on the one hand, of previously uttered messages and of those either already projected by the one speaker or anticipated as such by the other. But since each message is directed at someone, the context may also be said to consist of the interlocutors themselves, who in part determine what is uttered by the other – its formulation and manner of expression (intonation). For Bakhtin, not only does the subject lend specificity to his utterance, but so does another's anticipated or in fact articulated reaction, so that the single utterance is penetrated by the speaker's sense of the other, which contributes to establish its particular locus of meaning. Were there a different interlocutor or receiver of the message, in other words, that message might be formulated or enunciated differently. All dialogue thus takes cognizance of the other's previous and possible future utterances.

The utterance is deemed monological, however, if it does not take such cognizance, thereby affording no further possibility for dialogue. The author's word is then directed solely toward the referent and allows for no qualifying point of view. Similarly, the character's utterance is also 'single-voiced' if it is both characteristic and representative of him exclusively, serving the purely denotative purpose for which it is employed. In both instances, a single utterance predominates and does not assimilate any other. These represent independent utterances reflecting a single intention, ideology, or 'belief system'.

Contrastively, that word which is directed both toward the object and toward another's word is considered dialogical or 'double-voiced'. The dialogical word requires not only the presence of another but that the other's semantic position be assimilated into the speech of the subject, whose own utterance is at the same time attempting to take into account the other's intention. This is achieved when either another's language is incorporated into one's own speech, where it is accentuated according to the speaker's criteria and intentions, or when the language of the other – while not itself incorporated – is seen actively to influence the speaker's accentuation or semantic orientation. In all such instances, the word of the other – either from within the speaker's discourse or outside it – assists in determining the word of the self. Such is the case in literature and in life. But in verbal art there is an added dimension: 'Literature creates utterly specific images of people, where *I* and *another* are combined in a special and unrepeatable way: *I* in the form of *another* or *another* in the form of *I*. Thus encapsulated we find expressed the potential relationship of the author to his character in 'a dialogue of languages', whereby *'another's speech in another's language* [serves] to express authorial intentions but in a refracted way' (*PDP*, 293–4, 324). In this manner, through artistic expression and the fulfillment of aesthetic purpose, the confluence of the self and other, as author and hero, finds its 'special and unrepeatable' locus.

Within that locus, Bakhtin's distinction between one's own word and the alien word of the other is reduced, in effect, by the one discourse being assimilated and incorporated as part of the other discourse. The presence of the other person's word thus defines the concept of the dialogical word, where the intention of the one speaker is penetrated by that of the other, yielding 'an intersection of two consciousnesses'. Or, conversely: 'Consciousness is in essence multiple' (*PDP*, 289, 288). As noted, who speaks, what is said, and for whom the message is uttered represent a triad of crucial considerations. When viewed through the prism of Bakhtin's thinking, these concerns significantly alter the static conception of the semiotic model of human communication. That model provides for a sender, message, and receiver. But there is no indication of how the message is formulated – of what considerations go into its conception. Such static view may be revised in light of Bakhtin's dynamic perspective, according to which the message is conceived and articulated in consequence of what has already been uttered by the speaker and with regard to his possible future utterances, and in reaction to the previous utterances of an interlocutor, as well as in anticipation of that speaker's potential future responses not yet said.

Further, the message is determined by both speakers' conceptions of the object of discourse (or point of contention), which may, of course, not coincide. Yet, in the presence of the 'alien word', a positive perspective – fundamental to Bakhtin's thesis in its most global form – must nevertheless be acknowledged to apply. For in affirming spirit, Bakhtin repeatedly declares that 'The word (or in general any sign) is interindividual' (*SG*, 121), exist-

ing as a means of both self-expression and self-fulfillment.
It is therefore succinctly argued that in life ' "I" can realize
itself verbally only on the basis of "we"' (*Discourse*, 100),
while in narrative there exists the further 'possibility of
translating one's own intentions from one linguistic system to another . . . of saying "I am me" in someone else's
language, and in my own language, "I am other"' (*DI*,
315). By thus valorizing such 'translation' efforts, broadly
conceived as a source for both artistic creation and the
striving for mutual comprehension, the boundaries between the self and other are declared fluid and the possibility for cross-fertilization affirmed. Just as the word in
discourse is proclaimed to exist at the interstices between
the self and other, so is 'the artistic gift of form', in
extension of this notion, said to be actualized 'only on the
boundaries of two consciousnesses' (*Art*, 96–7). From this
perspective, affirming the collaborative nature of both
dialogue and art making, the articulation of an utterance
might itself be construed as a creative act, bearing the
potential for achieving an aesthetic effect.

In sum, in terms of its joint temporal and spatial features, time past and time future of both sender and receiver are in constant interaction within the articulated
message of the present. Moreover, the possible varying
conceptions of the referent on the part of the individual
speakers respectively, on the one hand, and the fundamental (social and other) distinctions between them, on
the other, are likewise enfused within the message as
crucial determining factors in its overall construction.
From the perspective of these interlocked, inherent considerations, the word or utterance is construed as being
formulated by the one speaker with constant regard to the
other and his word, but where both are intrinsically engaged in the production of the message. All such temporal
and spatial considerations derived from the thought of
Bakhtin might therefore be superimposed as interlocking
grids upon the conventional semiotic model of human
communication in an effort to transform its current static
conception into one that is dynamic and capable of regarding discourse as potential dialogue. In this fundamental

sense every word of the self would be viewed as dialogical in its potential to evoke a responsive word from the other, whose utterance in turn necessarily bears the same potential for initiating further discourse.

Conversely, as the negative correlative, which Bakhtin also addresses: 'A single person, remaining alone with himself, cannot make ends meet even in the deepest and most intimate spheres of his own spiritual life, he cannot manage without *another* consciousness. One person can never find complete fullness in himself alone' (PDP, 177). The fugitive effort to do so, one may assume, results in an approach that is resistant to dialogue. But the loss resulting from this monologic perspective is ultimately shared, since, in Bakhtin's broadly encompassing humanistic vision, the failing of the (self-proclaimed) authoritative self is perhaps the more tragic. 'The genuine life of the personality is made available only through a *dialogic* penetration of that personality, during which it freely and reciprocally reveals itself' (PDP, 59). Therefore, where there is restricted freedom and no reciprocation, one who denies the other and his potentially engaging word drastically reduces the possibility of spiritual fulfillment for himself primarily. The restriction of dialogical interaction thus bears a certain tragic potential, borne out repeatedly in the linked realms of the personal and political, where violence as a response – verbal or otherwise – represents the negative correlative of dialogue. And in this monologic, self-negating domain, in which the double-voiced word is essentially denied the right to be heard, the shared rich potential of the dialogically engaged self and other yields to what might be termed instead the self and object. By declaring the other, in effect, an object – or muted receiver – of the self's unresponsive authoritative word, the one reduces the other's as well as one's own self-fulfilling potential in the process.[1]

Meaning, then, in its most significant form as Truth, is created in dialogue, on the borders where two consciousnesses meet. It is realized at the interstices of the self and other, in affirmation of the notion that 'the reality of the word, as is true of any sign, resides between individuals'

(*MPL*, 14). Meaning as Truth may thus be said to belong to neither the self nor the other but inheres within an ideal third category, in which the word and intention of each are intermeshed but transcended. 'From the point of view of truth, there are no individual consciousnesses' (*PDP*, 81), writes Bakhtin, suggesting that someone's earlier fragmented 'truth' – as well as the disintegrative self – are potentially made whole, if only fleetingly, by the interaction of several viewpoints. Truth, in other words, belongs to no one; it is realized, rather, in the realm of dialogue, where the linked utterances of the self and other interpenetrate, yielding a truth which is fluid, ephemeral, and evanescent. Not only does it not reside with any*one*, but it is itself contextual, depending upon its temporal and spatial configuration, on the interlacing of the dialogic word of the self and other.

Although certain distinctions are clearly evident between the self and other in the joint domains of art and life, the aesthetic realm, for Bakhtin, extends into all realms. There is no distinct border between art and life. The one seeps into the unbounded confines of the other in an ongoing process of mutual reflection and cross-fertilization. When projected into these two joint domains, the complex notion of self and other refracts into a potentially infinite series of prismatic, kaleidoscopic impressions that are ever-shifting and regrouping, but remain interlocked in the linked correspondences of author–hero, contemplator–contemplated, the actual and fictional, writer–text, and text–reader. From among these, certain roles may be immediately reversed, interchange, or co-occur. In postulating the self as contemplator and the other as contemplated, for instance, the two will demonstrate an obviously fluid exchange of roles. Less apparent, perhaps, is the case of the author and reader. For the former, as one possibility, the reader may be conceived as the 'ideal' receiver of a coded message. As other, in this sense, he represents the writer's projected or imagined psychological construct. But in the more concrete circumstances of author and reader their roles are similarly interchangeable, since the writer, of necessity, both during and presumably after the writing process becomes a reader of his own work. As writer, he must read, reflect upon, and criticize the work in progress. Such endeavor is, in essence, the work of the other. Conversely, the reader slips into his 'opposite' complementary role upon taking up the pen, in order to respond as critic.

Certain considerations, however, do remain fixed. For instance, the other is seen to exist totally and exclusively in time and space by the self (and vice versa). Yet the *I* exists within that outer domain and within its own inner world as well (where its primary life-long task is to create and recreate itself as a meaningful – or meaning-bearing – well-integrated psychological and spiritual being). The consciousness of the self thus spans two worlds: the outer, determined by its relevant temporal and spatial coordinates – its place in the world, in other words – and the inner, where it attempts to find its 'place' within its self. One's own unity is therefore one of meaning derived from incorporating the inner world of the self; the other's unity appears only as a spatial–temporal unity. From the perspective of the self, then, the other exists only within the single outer plane of time and space. There is no way, clearly, for the self to experience directly the inner plane of the other. Yet, paradoxically, it is only the self that is capable of actualizing or giving form to the (outer *and* inner) world of the other – on another plane entirely: the fictional or aesthetic.

In this sense, as Bakhtin declares, all of the books in the world are written about the other and for the other. An aesthetic approach to the world means, therefore, perceiving it as the world of others who have previously lived their life in it. Once completed, when the limits are given, then an aesthetic conception of that life can be imaged and formed within those limits. 'To be artistically interested is to be interested, independently of meaning, in a life that is in principle consummated' (*Art*, 112). But in order to engage in the process of creation in the first place, the author must inevitably project his inner self and corresponding language use outward, as it were, to form a conception of the hero and his mode of expression. Finally, upon completion, he remains in the role of contemplator, while the completed work becomes the fixed object (made whole) of his – and others' – contemplation.

Just as the author of a text must project himself as other to his fictional world, the self in the actual world is viewed by Bakhtin as consistently other to that world. Defined and oriented by its 'inner self-activity', the *I* is constrained to confront the outside world as an object, by which it cannot be contained. The self is thus intimately associated with its 'inner, world-exceeding activity', which in and of itself is defined as an aesthetic enterprise, since it implies the ongoing process of authoring the self. The other, by contrast, is inherently implicated with the outer world. What this means, on the one hand, is that the other serves as prism through which the world is refracted for the self. However, that same prism affords the *I*, in turn, its only refracted vision of itself.

In the absence of that other, in Bakhtin's view, 'a human being experiencing life in the category of his own *I* is incapable of gathering himself on his own into an even relatively finished outward whole'. The constituent features of the self as an open, unfinished entity may be said to be 'authored' by the self, but all the same it is not given to the *I* to experience that entity in an immediate manner. Rather, this can be accomplished, in part, only by the mediating efforts of the other. Further, in engaging in more than a mere attempt at self-contemplation, Bakhtin asserts: 'It is only in the other human being, in fact, that a living, aesthetically (and ethically) convincing experience of human finitude is given to me . . .' (*Art*, 36). Conversely, the self plays the same role – and is consequently of equal import – for the other, since 'Only the other's action is capable of being artistically understood and formed by me. . . . Only the other is *embodied* for me axiologically and aesthetically' (*Art*, 45, 51). What that means, again, is that the self is not 'embodied' for itself as an object of perception and evaluation but rather for others to accomplish the task.

This recognition contributes an explanation, in Bakhtin's terms, as to why man makes art. He does so in order to experience immediately and directly, with no outside intermediary or auxiliary, a creation that is his and that he *can* experience in such direct fashion. Although man is partially perceptible to himself (largely through the mediation of another), his own self remains in constant flux and resultant fragmentary (psycho-spiritual) form in a world which is likewise fragmented and indeterminate. But his own creative work, by also being other to him (and he with respect to it), is therefore susceptible to being immediately contemplated – and, ideally, even evaluated – by him. Art, in this sense, may be the one invaluable luxury that man cannot afford to do without.

AUTHOR AND HERO

In the work of verbal art what is presented for perception and contemplation is both self-contained and whole. Since the text in which the hero resides is bound and fixed by its creator, the information provided the reader is all he will ever come to know. But in the epistemologically and axiologically unbounded region of life (as Bakhtin would put it) – that is, in a world where the potential for knowledge and the values derived from that knowledge are both unlimited – additional information may always be garnered or will surface of its own, making for new value systems or changes in the old. Cultural codes, in other words, do not remain fixed. In contrast to the work of art which is conclusively defined by its self-contained, bounded nature, the 'event of lived life' is precluded from eventually being made whole. What can be known of the other in life is likewise always partial and truncated. Forever dissolving at the periphery and reforming itself in an ever-changing state of flux, that event produces an endless series of both externally and internally generated transformations. As the subject of contemplation, the other is thus resilient and changing in constant interaction with an open, indeterminate world. The same, of course, may be said of the self.

Regarding the more specific but deceptively simple designation of the self as author, Bakhtin distinguishes, first, between the author–creator and the author-as-person in a number of respects. As 'a constitutive moment of the work', the status of the former is relegated to the past upon completion of the text. The notion of author–creator for a given work thus effectively dissolves, leaving in its stead the author–person as 'a constitutive moment of the ethical, social event of life', who may then offer insights into the work from decidedly different perspectives than formerly – as critic, psychologist, or even moralist. In the special instance of the author rendering autobiographical material, there evolves a separate and individual case, in which the author 'must become another in relation to himself . . .' (*Art*, 15). However, in general, if there is to be an 'aesthetic event', then the presence of 'an actively contemplating spectator' is needed by the self (as author–creator) to make possible that event.

In the making of verbal art, the relationship of the author to his hero confirms that supposition, since the author's role is posited as being dual in this sense: first, he must be other to his hero in the creation of him; but, upon completion of the artistic endeavor, he becomes a contemplator of his creation. In both roles, however, the creative and the contemplative, there emerges a (created) consciousness outside of the author that allows for the making of the hero and his world into a 'completable whole' in the first place. The author thus enters into the consciousness of his subject, and in doing so 'consummates' – through the creative process – the character's existence on the fictional plane. Bakhtin projects this process, essentially, as the task of translating oneself from an inner language into the language of 'outward expressedness'. In this sense, the making of verbal art amounts to a translation process from 'inner' thought to 'outward' manifestation, as a transference of (certain aspects of) the self to an other. Having accomplished this goal, the author then relinquishes his creative role in favor of a contemplative one which, in Bakhtin's scheme of things, is also both 'active and productive'. The making of an aesthetic *whole* thus requires the active contribution of an author–creator and author–contemplator. However, just as the concepts of self and other are interchangeable, essentially as 'shifters', so are these two initially linked authorial roles transferable to the sphere of the reader, who also creates, or 'co-creates' the work, which he at the same time contemplates.

As the originator and guarantor of the artistic work as a fully conceived whole, the author achieves his goal through what Bakhtin terms 'transgradience'. This may be defined as the quality of being in a potentially empathetic relationship (as both concerned 'insider' and, of necessity, 'outsider') to the other (as character or hero). Motivated as a well-intentioned orientation toward guidance and organizational activity in an essentially unequal partnership (where the one member is privy to greater insight or knowledge than his less-informed counterpart), the concept constitutes a basic factor in Bakhtin's philosophy of the interaction between the self and other in both art and life. It is manifested as a teleologically oriented activity, in which the one demonstrates a fundamental interest and concern for the other, through one consciousness temporarily inhabiting another as a means of achieving definition and (artistic) fulfillment for the latter. The domain of transgradient activity, as a catalyst for positive change or unification within diversity, includes the dialogic interaction between individuals, but may also extend from the realm of the actual to the fictional through the author's sympathetic endeavor to make not only the hero's consciousness – but his entire fictional universe – whole.

This is achieved by virtue of the fact that the author knows what each of his characters knows, and more, but instills in them an integrity and fullness of knowing based exclusively on what is definitively made a part of their purview. Within such restricted but well-defined epistemological limits, their interaction affords the literary work the sense of being a fully conceived entity. Being in a position of intensive 'outsideness' with respect to his hero, the author as guiding consciousness is able, first, to 'assemble' his hero's disparate features; second, to make of that assemblage an artistically conceived unity; and, finally, in consequence of these efforts, to consummate his hero's life story as bearing an integrity of its own fully independent of all other (extra-aesthetic) considerations. Yet, paradoxically, these considerations – what Bakhtin calls the 'givenness of lived life' – await their reformulation or recreation as newly formed objects posited by art that provide the wholeness or boundedness that art seeks (but always necessarily fails) to make of life. What is given in the world must therefore be transmuted through artistic endeavor to the aesthetic plane, where the goal is to bring forth a fully integrated perspective.

In elaborating the relationship of the author to his hero, Bakhtin constantly shifts his discussion from the plane of the fictional to the actual world. Oddly, he frequently refers to the character in a work as a human being, bearing a biography akin to the author and, therefore, as being the bearer of his own destiny. But in the repeated shift from the fictional to the actual, he consistently points to the fact that the 'life' of the character is conceived and made whole in a way that is non-coincident with what happens in life. For just as the event of a lived life is 'a unity incapable of being consummated from within itself', similarly 'our own consciousness would never say to itself the word that would consummate it' (*Art*, 14, 16–17). That, after all, is the job of the other. And, in performing that task, through the creative process, the author is able to provide in a selfless transgradient act the consummating word required for his hero. In result, 'The aesthetic act gives birth to being on a new axiological plane of the world: a new human being is born and a new axiological context – a new plane of thinking about the human world' (*Art*, 191).

What the creative process amounts to is one of projection and translation (of inner 'language' into outer expressedness) on the part of the author, resulting in the transformation of an object into some new form. By aesthetically experiencing the other, the author in effect transmutes that other into an aesthetic object to be further contemplated as hero. The author's relationship to his character may thus be understood as 'the author's *creative* reaction to the hero and his life', where the author is the 'form-giver', while the concept of form itself is conceived as a *'boundary* that has been wrought aesthetically' (*Art*, 90). That creation is achieved as the result of what Bakhtin calls 'sympathetic understanding' on the part of the author, in response to the object in its original extra-aesthetic form. For the way in which form is given is from without, by a consciousness which is aware of another potential 'consciousness', upon which the author–creator works his form-giving vision, yielding, ultimately, the work of art as a clearly defined whole.

Bakhtin conveys the notion of wholeness by observing that the beginning and end of a life are not experienced by the self but can only be empathetically experienced by some other outside of the self. In life the birth and death of the self as (opening and closing) facts are encompassed by the life experience of the other exclusively. Thus, 'my own life is that which temporally encompasses the existence of others. . . . my own boundaries . . . are never given to me and . . . are in principle incapable of being experienced by me' (*Art*, 105). One's own life can therefore only be conceived as a whole (as having a beginning and an end) through the outside perception and sympathetic understanding of the other, who records and consummates the figure of the self in an aesthetically significant image or artistic configuration. Analogously, one cannot experience one's own face without some form of mediation (a mirror, a photograph, or painting) on the cognitive plane. Nor, as Bakhtin points out, can one forgive oneself for one's own sins on some (as he claims, non-existent) axiological plane. But, on the aesthetic plane, the concept of sympathetic understanding and its eventual correspondent 'translation' allows for the possibility of transmuting life into art – of making what cannot be whole to the self, whole through the form-giving efforts of the self as other. In result, within this productive, generative framework, the dialogic word is articulated and the artistic text created.

For Bakhtin, as noted, another's discourse in general represents a largely unrecognized but main topic of discourse itself in both literature and life. The related concerns of how the word of the other is transmitted and what effect is produced thereby are seen as crucial to the study of narrative especially. At the same time it is regarded as axiomatic that in every prose style there is an element of inner polemic expressed to some degree, as certain 'anticipated objections, evaluations, points of view' (*PDP*, 196) are taken into account. Hence the character's speech may express a point of view either entirely reflective of the author's, only partially so, or diametrically opposed to it. Yet within this schematic but all-inclusive range of possibility, the character is made to articulate an ideology that is his alone.

A character is born first to speak and only later, perhaps, to act (although in a crucial sense, for Bakhtin, to speak *is* to act). Expressed thus, the word in the abstract and its immanent potential for dialogue are again privileged. This potential finds its most profound realization, in Bakhtin's view, in the works of Dostoevsky, where the word of the author and his character are seen to exist on the same plane of importance. In the special case of the other as narrator, that fictional construct may be conceived similarly as bearing its own distinctive language, with the speech of the narrator not to be equated with the author's ideological viewpoint. The position of the one remains distinct from the other. But, within the author's perspective, there is the possibility for what Bakhtin calls 'nondirect speaking', which allows for verbal expression 'not *in* language but *through* language, through the linguistic medium of another – and consequently through a refraction of authorial intentions' (*DI*, 313). This is achieved, again, by the author's projection and translation of the self into the other as narrator or hero.

Within the framework of Bakhtin's critical distinction between one's own word and the alien word of the other, their dialogic engagement appears most evident when the latter is necessarily assimilated as part of the former. In such case, the utterance of a single speaker does not only take cognizance of that of the other but may make (direct or ironic) use of it as well. As reported speech and as a source of possible polemic, the word of the other penetrates that of the speaker, lending it a certain specificity and emphasis, while affording the discourse itself its dialogic quality. In considering such phenomena with regard to author and hero, Bakhtin specifies, from among three possible types of reported speech, 'quasi-direct discourse', as that which 'permits another's inner speech, to merge in an organic and structured way, with a context belonging to the author' (*DI*, 319).[2] In such instances, from one perspective, 'the boundaries of the message reported are maximally weakened' (*MPL*, 122), so that the speech and intonation of the author and character become virtually indistinguishable. The question of point of view here remains problematic, while the text challenges and defies the reader to identify which voice predominates. Yet from another perspective – the dialogical – the reader is witness to the near perfect merging of the self and other in verbal art. Such merging, moreover, affords the reader the clearest recognition of the fluidity of the boundaries between art and life, and the self and other.

In Bakhtin's view, in fact, the notion of such boundaries existing at all amounts to a misconception of the true nature of their interrelations. All of the seeming abstract considerations of the present discussion are instead thoroughly intertwined. The result of their intermeshing is what Bakhtin calls the 'three domains of human culture – science, art, and life' (*Art*, 1). Time and space are thus not the only aspects of the world which are inherently interrelated. Rather, as perhaps seemingly irreconcilable juxtaposed coordinates, both art and life, and the self and other, flourish jointly as catalysts for further mutual investigation and supportive development. Each is formative of and reflected in its respective counterpart; each specifies and is grounded in the other. There is no art without life, and no life without art. Similarly, the self and the word of the self are in part determined by the other, just as the other and his word are determined by the self. Nothing and no one exists independently. *In potentia*, man, his world, and his art are all of a piece – so long as we accept the responsibility that entails.

Part II

5

The Prague School Connection

MONOLOGUE AND DIALOGUE

Nearly half a century ago, in an article titled 'Dialogue and Monologue', Jan Mukařovský, the Prague School literary theorist and aesthetician, declared that 'The problem of the relationship between monologue and dialogue is one of the urgent questions of contemporary poetics . . .' (1977:81). Although 'contemporary poetics' has since made great strides (at times in a variety of mutually opposed directions), that problem remains only partly resolved today – and that due largely to the writings of Bakhtin. The distinctions Bakhtin makes between the two concepts, however, are derived at times from a sphere that embraces both metaphysical and ethical concerns, in which questions of dialogic relations nonetheless remain paramount. At the core of Bakhtin's entire philosophical thought, in fact, is the problem of 'dialogism', with its attendant complexities and difficulties. Yet the term appears both ill-defined and overburdened, and, as Michael Holquist remarks: 'Bakhtin himself must bear part of the responsibility for the widespread confusion that characterizes appropriations of "dialogism"' (*SG*, xiii). That confusion is not likely to be dispelled soon, but a clear limning of the problem is surely needed for its eventual resolution.

To respond (however belatedly) to Mukařovský's call of nearly half a century ago to distinguish meaningfully between monologue and dialogue would serve well as a first step. However, when Bakhtin's thinking is necessarily taken into account, the problem immediately becomes more complex than Mukařovský appears to have

77

envisioned, since it must then be extended beyond the realm of poetics, to which the Czech thinker would have seen it applied. It also extends, however, beyond Bakhtin's own translinguistics. Encompassing the complexities of dialogical relations in literary texts, that projected new discipline is conceived to incorporate more broadly the related concerns of everyday discourse as well. However, ideological considerations that are central to Bakhtin's metaphysics further complicate as well as enhance the matter of distinguishing between monologue and dialogue. That question, it seems, is thereby superseded by the need to distinguish between monologism and dialogism, as more broadly encompassing rubrics that extend beyond the sphere of discourse analysis (in literature and life) to that of ideology, as it pertains to these two modes of discourse. Hence the problem as Mukařovský originally posed it becomes more complex even as it remains essentially unresolved. The intention here and in the final chapter will be to approach the question both from the standpoint of literary and quotidian speech, as well as from the attendant ethical viewpoint that Bakhtin also proposes.

Mukařovský regards monologue and dialogue as two mutually opposed elementary attitudes, whose relation is characterized by a 'dynamic polarity' which affords one or the other predominance at any given moment within speech activity. In this constantly renewed struggle for primacy, emphasis is placed on the relationship between speaker and listener, 'the active and passive subject', as Mukařovský conceives of the complementary roles exhibited by the participants in discourse. Monologue is thus defined as 'an utterance with a single active participant regardless of the presence or absence of other passive participants' (1977:81, fn.1). All that is needed for monologue to take place, in other words, is a single speaker who may be the only one present to hear his own words. (As Bakhtin abbreviates it in his later, unfinished writings: 'Monologue as speech that is addressed to no one and does not presuppose a response' (*SG*, 117). Further, in conformity with Prague School thinking, Mukařovský posits the alternation of speech between two speakers as fundamental to dialogue. Accordingly, the dialogic mode requires that the speakers undertake roles that are alternately active and passive. This feature, for Mukařovský, represents the principal opposition at play in the distinction between monologue and dialogue. Although further distinctions have been made by other Prague School thinkers between 'monologue and dialogue language', this terminological distinction appears both fruitless and unproductive, as though in either case a certain specific lexicon were employed. While such a viewpoint serves to heighten the sense of a distinction between monologue and dialogue, it does little to inspire a clear sense of the principal differences between them.

By emphasizing an interlocutor's role as either active or passive, Mukařovský considers that in monologue one participant is consistently active, the other passive, 'whereas in dialogue the roles constantly change: each of the two subjects is alternately active and passive' (Ibid.: 96). In the precedence given to dialogue by the Czech thinker, one of its basic defining aspects is determined by the participants' changing respective attitudes toward what is being articulated. Posited 'as a special kind of semantic structure oriented toward a maximum of semantic reversal' (Ibid.: 109), the dialogic mode affords the possibility for change and a developing point of view. In this crucial respect, Mukařovský's discussion conforms with Bakhtin's similar appreciation of dialogue as a potential catalyst for development and growth. Yet the Czech theorist argues generally that dialogue is composed of interlarded monologic statement, essentially reaffirming the position taken by the Prague School in its 1929 'Theses', wherein the distinction is made between 'alternately interrupted (dialogic) speech and unilaterally uninterrupted (monologic) speech' (Steiner 1982:12). But this is only adequate as a static description, which fails to account for the possible manner or cause by which speech is either 'interrupted' or, as an equally critical consideration, left 'unilaterally uninterrupted'. These concerns, after all, presuppose the need for a more concentrated focus upon the relation, influence, and verbal exchange between the interlocutors themselves and their respective utterances. With respect to which speaker predominates at any given moment and to what degree the one articulated position is affected or ameliorated by the other's stated views, the linked principles of alternation and change are heralded as prominent features of dialogue. Yet the main focus remains concentrated upon the participants themselves and their roles. Mukařovský also acknowledges, however, 'the potential dialogic nature of every utterance' (Ibid.: 109), a view which is in clear agreement with Bakhtin's argument that the fundament of dialogue is potentially present in a single word, since the word – as the basic unit of discourse – 'is by its very nature dialogic' (*PDP*, 183).

In other critical respects, however, the views of the two contemporaries appear not to coincide. Mukařovský is primarily concerned with the subjects, their roles and attitudes; Bakhtin's emphasis, by contrast, falls equally upon the utterance and its unique aspect within any given context. While the Czech theoretician regards the roles of the participants as alternately active and passive, for Bakhtin such a view is simplistic. Rather than take an exclusively passive role at any time – even when one speaker is resolutely silent – the two subjects consistently influence one another's speech. Neither participant ever engages in an entirely passive role, since each as a matter of course directs his speech toward the other, and takes the latter's character, social position, relation to the speaker and similar related facets into consideration prior to articulating a single word. To be dialogically engaged, in Bakhtin's terms, means for the utterance of the one to penetrate the utterance of the other and thereby partially determine its form and meaning. This latter contention leads, in effect, to the obscuring of the boundary – but not the distinction – between the two modes of discourse. What appears to be what is commonly termed 'monologue' may well bear a dialogical component as well.

As a further point of divergence, whereby the one thinker emphasizes the speaking subject and the other his word, Mukařovský concentrates upon the potentially changing attitude of the interlocutor to the theme of discourse, but is not concerned with the message and its relation to the referent – whether it be emphatically denotative and unyielding in its acknowledged perspective, or more attenuated in its stated position and therefore susceptible to the argument of another possible viewpoint. In this respect as well the utterance is deemed less significant than its user. Also incongruent, from Bakhtin's perspective, is Mukařovský's emphasis upon the principle of alternation, whereby both monologue and dialogue are seen as being engaged in a constant struggle for temporary predominance. In an elementary effort to discern the *'dialogic quality'* (1977:109) potentially evident in monologue, Mukařovský shows dialogue to be composed of interlarded monologic statement. Bakhtin is concerned, by contrast, to reveal the mutually contradictory influences embroiled within a single speech act. Thus the notion of the alternation between monologue and dialogue, defined in terms of a presumed active or passive role exhibited by the participants, is, for Bakhtin, inadequate. Rather, each interlocutor potentially contributes to dialogue, even when silent.

*

In elaborating Mukařovský's 1940 study, a contemporary Prague School apologist observes that some of the characteristic features of 'dialogue language' include 'the first and second grammatical persons constantly changing places . . . shifts and reversals of meaning, the integration of whatever is said in two or more alternating and interpenetrating semantic contexts, differentiation of the utterances according to various personal vocabularies, ways of speaking, dialects, and so on'. But, as the crucial concern, it is unequivocally stated (again in conformity with Mukařovský in particular and with Prague School thinking in general) that 'to be read as dialogue, a literary text or segment of a text must be divided into alternating speeches attributed to different speakers'. Curiously, the same researcher takes Bakhtin to task when he observes that, in his book on Dostoevsky, Bakhtin 'completely overlooked the crucial importance of the division into speeches when he qualified Dostoevsky's "polyphonic" novel as a true dialogue' (Veltruský 1984:599). While that particular censure appears quite undistinguished, Bakhtin does in fact define dialogue in just such fashion – and also in clear conformity with the basic definition proposed by the Prague School – when he declares:

> The boundaries of each concrete utterance as a unit of speech communication are determined by a *change of speaking subjects*, that is, a change of speakers. . . . One observes this change of speaking subjects most simply and clearly in actual dialogue where the utterances of the interlocutors or partners in dialogue . . . alternate. (*SG*, 71, 72)

Moreover, in the telegraphic manner of a later, unfinished essay, he acknowledges the same basic suppositions but hints, significantly, at their entirely elementary character:

> The narrow understanding of dialogue as one of the compositional forms of speech (dialogic and monologic speech). One can say that each rejoinder in and of itself is monologic (the absolutely minimal monologue) and each monologue is a rejoinder from a larger dialogue . . . (*SG*, 117)

Dialogue is thus conceived on a fundamental level as being composed of interlarded monologic speech elements. But to suggest that 'the division into speeches delivered by alternating interlocutors [is] the ultimate criterion of what is a dialogue and what is not' (Veltruský 1984:599), goes but a short distance in providing an understanding of what intricacies are at work in eliciting and maintaining dialogical interaction.

Thus, while crediting that fundamental description of dialogue as alternating speech, Bakhtin argues further, as a way of elucidating those intricacies, that in dialogue neither speaker is ever passive, whether speaking or not.

Rather, each is consistently engaged at all times in an effort to convince, rebutt, or refute the other, while constantly modifying his position with respect to what has so far been articulated and in anticipation of what might yet be said. Bakhtin's emphasis, in contrast to the Prague School thinker, is therefore jointly focused upon both the speaker *and* the utterance, acknowledging thereby the preeminent role played by the latter in eliciting (further) dialogue. Such emphasis upon not only the role of the speakers but upon that of their respective word serves to focus more sharply upon the complexity of dialogic interaction. For it goes beyond the simplistic recognition of heralding alternating speech as the fundamental dialogical principle, by acknowledging the internal dynamics at play, at each respective pivotal moment, when one speaker's utterance serves to evoke a new considered dialogic response from the other.

Taken a seeming paradoxical step further, for Bakhtin, not only is dialogue carried on between two speakers, whose speech is characterized by responsive alternation. There is also the potential for dialogue between what C.S. Peirce calls 'different phases of the ego', specifying, in Bakhtinian terms, the potential dialogical relationship of the speaker to his own utterances. Bakhtin would surely subscribe as well (as noted) to Peirce's dictum that 'All thinking is dialogic in form'. However, where others speak simply of interior monologue, Bakhtin refers to 'a thoroughly dialogized interior monologue', which he terms 'interior dialogue' (*PDP*, 74), a distinction that bears further consideration. For this raises the question of whether – beyond the previously noted 'narrow understanding' of each rejoinder in dialogue being 'in and of itself monologic' – there exists any such thing as monologue? Or is it, rather, always the case of a single being – at the least – engaging in dialogue either with himself (as a constantly changing 'ego') or with others in responsive exchange that effectively eliminates all concept of monologue except as interlarded speech fragments? Such would appear to be a reasonable conclusion from the perspective of Peirce and, oddly, for Bakhtin as well.

Because so much of Bakhtin's thought depends on at least the implied opposition between monologue and dialogue, it indeed appears paradoxical that the former concept may seem to dissolve in formulations revealing it as ultimately chimerical. That suspected chimerical aspect may of course be salvaged by simply acknowledging (with Bakhtin) that monologue, in its narrow sense, appears as an alternating fragment of dialogue. (What Bakhtin has to say about the 'monologic word' *per se* and about 'monologism', as an unacceptable strategy, constitutes a related but separate topic that will be treated later.) Nonetheless, in rejecting the notion of monologue existing as a separate, self-contained speech entity, an argument may be advanced in which 'inner speech' is claimed to be the core feature of consciousness as well as being inherently dialogical in nature. Derived from the writings of Voloshinov, concerning inner speech, we read that ultimately no act of consciousness is possible without it. . . . Any awareness needs *inner* speech, inner *intonation* and a rudimentary inner style. . . . Consciousness, unless it is embodied in the ideological material of the inner word, gesture, sign or symbol, does not and cannot exist. . . . Without inner speech there can be no consciousness, just as there is no outer speech without inner speech' (*BSP*, 105, 107, 108, 111). Proceeding beyond the notion of inner speech being immanent to consciousness, in that final observation it is viewed as the core element of 'outer speech' as well. From there to saying that there is essentially no functional difference between inner and outer speech is but a short step.

That step is taken when we are told that since 'inner speech . . . is broken down into separate repliques of varying size . . . it takes the form of dialogue' (*BSP*, 119). Buttressed by the principle that any given speech (even that 'talk' that we have with ourselves) is rendered in the expectation of some kind of response, what is seemingly monologic, according to this line of thought, appears also to be dialogic. Given Bakhtin's (and the Prague School's) basic oppositional ploy of setting off 'monologue and dialogue speech', our efforts at resolving the problem come full circle in the claim that 'all speech is dialogic speech, directed at another person, at his *understanding* and at his real or potential *response*' (*BSP*, 122). While the potential for dialogue is thus declared an inherent, definitive aspect of language, as Bakhtin believed, the concept of monologue remains relegated to an abstract inconclusive realm characterized by what remains essentially an unresolved ambiguity.

MONOLOGISM AND DIALOGISM

Inherent in the distinction between monologue and dialogue, Bakhtin also elaborates broadly a concern that is both ethical and metaphysical. Whereas the Prague School distinguishes between 'dialogic speech and monologic speech', neither, it would seem, is granted a privileged ideological position. In Bakhtin's system of thought, wherein he calls for 'surmounting monologism', such is not the case. Instead, the value attached to 'monologism' is potentially negative rather than neutral and is diametrically opposed, in principle, to dialogue. Defined by and dependent upon its outwardly derived authority, the monologic word stands in opposition to the 'living' dialogic word, which is vitalized and constantly revivified by its varied contextual usage and by the rich abundance of meanings that as a result accrue to it.

In stark contrast, Bakhtin declares, 'What monologism is, in the highest sense, [is] a denial of the equal rights of consciousnesses vis-à-vis truth . . .' (*PDP*, 285) By denying those 'rights' monologism may appear in its most extreme (political) form as violence – as the triumph of might rather than the word. In this sense, the potentially bountiful relationship between the self and other – as vital links in the chain of human communication – necessarily breaks down, since the word as an otherwise dynamic ideological source is reduced to the level of an unproductive stasis. That the authoritative word itself, as inert object, will inevitably be deprived of its authority may be presumed as certain as the fact that the political, economic, and social fortunes to which it is bound are sure to change. Likewise, the reduction of the potentially dialogic utterance to its monologic counterpart is certain to affect negatively the communicative chain. For in providing the occasion for such reduction, the one claiming an unassailable position in effect substitutes for the truth-seeking dialogic word a rigidified verbal construct that masks and obfuscates, rather than communicates.

In sum, the Prague School definitions of monologue and dialogue may have appeared inadequate, especially in light of the problems that Bakhtin raises. However, in attempting to get beyond its seemingly simplistic approach to the problem of definition, and by instituting instead the related concepts of monologism and dialogism, we find that the former term (with its moral and ethical implications) is relatively manageable conceptually, even though it is, in effect, a dead-end concept that Bakhtin would surely say leads us nowhere, except to the shutting down of dialogue, a negative potential to be deplored.

On the other hand, to anticipate, common appropriations of dialogism, while seeming to afford grand possibilities, may tend to overextend this rich concept in usage that ranges beyond the concrete understanding of dialogue as an engagement *between individuals* – that is, the understanding of the Prague School – to figurative formulations that allow us commonly to equate dialogism with intertextuality. So Yury Lotman, for instance, and virtually everyone else today, speaks of texts as engaging in 'dialogues and polylogues' (1974:304). And yet, if we could resurrect for a moment one of the Prague School thinkers, he might articulate in a perhaps strained whisper that only individuals engage in dialogue, not texts.

THE WORD AND THE WORK

Bakhtin's pioneering approach to the word as potential dialogical material is paralleled by Mukařovský's similarly pathbreaking recognition regarding the work of art as sign. Beginning with the common assumption that the sign stands for something other than itself, Mukařovský declares the artistic work a sign in his seminal 1934 essay, 'Art as a Semiotic Fact' (1978:82–8), by affirming both the semiotic and social aspects inherent in the execution and subsequent apperception and evaluation of the work. He contends that the referent of this highly proliferated but always *sui generis* sign is dependent upon both the encoder's intention, imperfectly understood at best, and the decoder's reception and interpretation, informed by his understanding and personal life experience. 'What he called "external stimuli" enter the artistic system through the intermediacy of the individual, through both the encoder and successive generations of decoders. There is projected into the work of art the psychological energy, or intentionality of both encoders and decoders, binding the components of a work into a semantic cohesiveness' (Winner and Winner 1976:148). The message is thus conceived as a variable dependent upon its continued and necessarily different reception by innumerable receivers in subsequent periods. This conception is formulated by Mukařovský as a 'global reference' that the artistic work effects by entering into 'a relationship with the entire world as reflected in the life experiences of persons, either senders or receivers' (1976:162). Hence the seemingly unending processes of semiosis or sign interpretation, envisioned by C.S. Peirce, is achieved with respect to aesthetic perception through the interaction of a single encoder with a virtually infinite host of potential decoders, while the work itself serves as an intermediary that is always inevitably perceived differently.

That encapsulated view asserts both the semiotic and related social aspect of the artistic work. Concerning the latter feature, for Mukařovský, the dominant aesthetic function of the artistic work is manifested within a social context which dictates the norms to which the work is subject. (Whether the artist affirms or rejects those norms remains a separate matter entirely.) In emphasizing 'the social importance of aesthetic phenomena' (1970:23), the Czech thinker declares that the artistic work 'is a sign, and hence at bottom is a social fact', while aesthetic value 'is basically a social phenomenon' (ibid.: 83, 95), and thus repeatedly acknowledges that aesthetic values within a culture are socially determined. Likewise, within an all-pervasive argument asserting 'the social life of the verbal sign' (*MPL*, 21) and its internal dialogical nature, we read (as previously cited) that 'the reality of the word, as is true of any sign, resides between individuals. . . . The sign is a creation between individuals, a creation within a social milieu' (*MPL*, 14, 22). The social significance of the word is thus likewise affirmed in thinking to which Bakhtin adheres since the word is seen to bear meaning only in dialogic interaction among its users. Mukařovský asserts essentially the same view with regard to the artistic work. Accordingly, the social aspect of dialogical interaction with regard to the word, in the one instance, and to the artistic work, in the other, is affirmed, respectively, by each thinker.

In considering the social aspect of dialogic relations, the concept of 'social evaluation', defined as 'the ideological purview of a given social group at some particular time' (Titunik 1973:183), comes into play in the thought of the Bakhtin circle as the vehicle by which a word acquires its special meaning, turning 'a grammatical possibility into a concrete fact of speech reality' (Medvedev 1978:123). In like manner, Mukařovský proposes the concept (borrowed from Saussure) of 'collective awareness', intended to convey the idea of a system of value judgments, in which 'value is perceived as existing independently of the will of an individual and his subjective decisions' (1970:25). However, there is an apparent difference in stress between the two concepts. The idea of 'social evaluation' may be adequately expressed in terms of human relations, emphasizing both the personal and the interpersonal: thus, '*Individual* emotions can come into play as *overtones* accompanying the *basic tone of social evaluation*. "I" can realize itself verbally only on the basis of "We"' (*Discourse*, 100). While a function of society as a whole, the notion of social evaluation may be understood to encompass that society's individual members engaged in dialogical interaction.

On the other hand, Mukařovský's 'collective awareness' is defined 'as the locus of existence of individual *systems* of cultural phenomena such as language, religion, science, politics' (1970:20; italics added). Each such system is social at base, just as collective awareness is itself a social fact. Whereas the one expression appears designed to accommodate the individual (and his word) as the microcosmic unit within a greater social sphere, Mukařovský's seems directed toward society's macrocosmic structures, where the interconnections among these individual systems results in a 'system of systems' (as it was termed in the period of late Formalism) or 'culture' (as it evolved in the usage of the Moscow–Tartu School). Such view allows for cross-fertilization within a series of either social structures primarily, or among individual utterances (within those structures) secondarily, but where the emphasis remains upon the structure rather than the utterance. As integrative of these two related perspectives, one might here recall the summative remark of the Formalist thinker, Lev Jakubinsky, who astutely observes that 'Dialogue . . . is without doubt a "cultural" phenomenon . . .' (cited in Mukařovský 1977:85), thereby encompassing the linkage between the individual and the social aspects of this 'phenomenon'.

As a principal representative of Czech structuralism, Mukařovský regards the literary or aesthetic work in terms of the relations of its parts to one another, to the whole, and to other structures outside the work. His emphasis upon relations acknowledges the complex exchange and interaction within structures, whose elements are engaged in complex interrelations, producing meaning. Accordingly, the concept of structure is designed to account for the dynamic interaction among constituent elements, yielding potentially new and meaningful information. Nowhere does that design hold truer than in the artistic text.

According to Mukařovský, the artistic text bears a communicative as well as an aesthetic function (1978:84–6), characterized by a 'dialectical antinomy' existing between the two.[1] In his view, the aesthetic function promotes a certain interaction between the subject (perceiver) and the aesthetic object (Mukařovský 1970:23), whereby the communicative function appears an inherent feature of the artistic sign. In evident accord with the Prague School thinker's position, contemporary thought of the Moscow–Tartu School likewise affirms that the literary text bears both an autonomous and a communicative character; art is characterized by a maximum of information, affording a corresponding high degree of organization. Moreover, in acknowledging that 'communication processes are a primary fact of human culture' (Shukman 1977:44), culture itself is perceived by the School as a phenomenon that exists as *collective memory* – that therefore relies upon the dialogical interaction of its members. Thus 'Culture . . . creates a social sphere around man which, like the biosphere, makes life possible; that is, not organic life, but social life' (Lotman and Uspensky 1978:213). Emphasis on the social aspect is further underscored by the observation that 'The function of a text is defined as its social role, its capacity to serve certain demands of the community which creates the text' (Lotman and Piatigorsky 1978:233).

That view affirming the social function of the text has its own brief history in twentieth-century East European thought. Introduced by Roman Jakobson and Jurij Tynjanov in a seminal 1928 essay, 'Problems in the Study of Literature and Language' (Matejka and Pomorska 1971: 79–81), the idea of 'system' is promoted in a set of theses that first challenges the early Formalist notion of the isolation of the work of art. Their joint statement affirms the interrelations of individual works and of the arts in general. Its concept of a 'system of systems' anticipates the work of Mukařovský, who posits a 'structure of structures', and that of Lotman, for whom 'culture' is a system of texts structurally and hierarchically related. The original intent of this joint position was to set in perspective extreme positions characteristic of the early, polemical period of Russian Formalism. In the frequently cited statement, the concept of the *immanence* of the work of art is superseded by the more balanced recognition of its *autonomy*, intended to acknowledge that the work exists in complex relations to other works and to 'systems' (or 'structures') understood as cultural institutions. In assessing the already expired Russian Formalist movement, Mukařovský declares (in reaction to the Formalists' earlier emphasis on the immanence or cultural isolation of the literary work) that while 'the postulate of autonomous development' must be retained, literature should not be deprived of 'its relations to the outside world' (1977:140). In like spirit, Lotman writes: 'The real flesh of the literary work consists of a text (a system of intratextual relations) *in its relationship to extratextual reality*: life, literary norms, tradition, ideas. It is impossible to conceive of *a text thoroughly extracted from this network*' (cited in Champagne 1978:206). In rejecting the early Formalist position regarding the work of art as entirely self-sufficient, immanent, and therefore separated from external reality, Mukařovský affirmed an incipient concept based on informational exchange that appears related to Bakhtin's concept of dialogism. From this standpoint, it is tempting to consider problems of aesthetics, including the social role of the work of art, in such 'dialogic' terms. Unwittingly succumbing to such 'temptation', Mukařovský asserts that 'in all its modifications art has much in common with a continuous *dialogue* in which both those who gradually create works, and those who perceive them, participate' (cited in Steiner 1978:xxxvi; italics added).[2]

Further, this same figurative thinking might be extended to parade under the banner of dialogism questions of the relation between aesthetic and extra-aesthetic spheres, a structure's interrelations with its constitutive parts, with other structures and cultural institutions, as well as the entire Formalist–structuralist 'debate', reformulated and interpreted in terms of a considered emphasis on a concept of dialogic exchange manifested on numerous levels. Broadly, such standpoint would adhere to those positions articulated during the period of late Formalism, Prague structuralism, and current semiotic thought, declaring a broad continuum of relations among individual artistic works and within the arts in general. Thus it may be argued that the idea of a system of systems (as a configuration of cultural institutions, including the arts, law, religion, and politics, among others) is both dialogic in its (figurative) essence and semiotic in scope, affirming that all aspects of human culture are interrelated sign systems, which are either intertextual in nature or correlational, with each supporting, refuting, lending substance to or borrowing from the other – *dialogically*. Yet at the same time it may be argued that such all-encompassing view places further undue burden on the already much appropriated concept of dialogism.

In discussing such cultural phenomena, all of which are regarded as being mutually interdependent and interconnected, Mukařovský considers that the various cultural systems, or institutions, are in a state of dialectical antinomy (1970:5), affording the potential for cross-fertilization between the aesthetic and extra-aesthetic realms, while he also acknowledges that such interchange 'promotes development in the entire area of aesthetics' (Ibid.: 24). In effect, Mukařovský's view corresponds on the macrocosmic plane of intracultural influence to Bakhtin's notion of the 'dialogic word', focused on the microcosmic level of human discourse. As Julia Kristeva puts it, 'By establishing the status of the word as *minimal unit* of the text, Bakhtin deals with structures at its deepest level . . .' (1980:88).[3] Mukařovský, on the other hand, concentrates on the entire culture as text or, better, on those individual systems composing the greater system or 'culture', where each such system potentially enters into informational exchange relations with other systems that are analogous to the dialogic relations of individual utterances. This view, moreover, corresponds to the Moscow–Tartu School's provisional definition of culture, in its well-known set of abbreviated 'Theses', as 'concerned with the processing, exchange, and storage of information' (Lotman *et al.* 1975:57).

In these related respects the present artificially constructed exchange between the Czech and Russian theorists has been employed in an attempt to define and further specify what has come to be celebrated (frequently without great elaboration) as the principle of dialogism. That 'principle' may be approached in terms that acknowledge the speakers and their roles, as well as the constitutive units of speech (the word, the utterance), whose immanent temporal and spatial attributes are singularly brought to bear in the creating and structuring of each instance of dialogue. However, in further employing Bakhtin's broadly applicable concept to include questions of textual and intertextual relations, and analogous interrelations affecting the entire cultural domain, like *specific* attributes need be defined and similarly applied. Analogous to those basic discursive units that are fundamental to Bakhtin's entire project, the concept of dialogism, encompassing that project, must be submitted to a like program of 'framing' – or of seeking definition – by which it may eventually *attain* its limits. For in such attainment that rich concept will achieve a more certain and justified application than we are capable of assigning it at present.

6

The Moscow–Tartu
School Connection

STRATEGIES OF FRAMING

In the thought of Bakhtin monologue occupies a precarious position. So much of his thinking depends on at least the implied opposition between monologue and dialogue. Yet we have been hard pressed to determine under just what conditions monologue – in his view – does in fact take place. In light of this apparent paradox, Bakhtin nonetheless acknowledges the importance of interlarded monologic speech as framed structures. Potentially whole unto themselves, but figuring as only part of a larger dialogue in which they are embedded, such speech elements constitute individual texts of varying scope and dimension. The opening and closing statements of an utterance are thus understood to represent the boundaries of speech that not only initiate and close an argument but also serve as points of tangency, as it were, between the speakers' utterances. Within these structures constituting dialogue, opening and closing statements are especially significant. 'For they are, so to speak, sentences of the "front line" that stand right at the boundary of the change of speech subjects' (*SG*, 89, fn. i). Therefore the question of what strategies go into the 'framing' of an utterance – that is, how the utterance is initiated and concluded, is deemed crucial to an understanding of dialogic speech.

This same concern is particularly appropriate when attempting to distinguish between the various modes of reported speech, especially when the category of quasi-direct speech comes into play. Properly defined as 'discourse that is formally authorial, but that belongs in its

95

"emotional structure" to a represented character, whose inner speech is transmitted and regulated by the author' (*SG*, 130, ed. fn. 15), quasi-direct discourse exhibits framed or embedded texts, whose frames are frequently difficult to discern, but which reveal relations that are dynamic precisely because more than one voice may be registered.

A heightened awareness of the making and breaking of frames applies not only to the problem of isolating and distinguishing between various narrative voices but also between shorter narratives, or subtexts, incorporated within the greater text. Thus, as one theorist suggests, 'the analyst must determine what shall count as the elementary units of narrative and investigate the ways in which they combine' (Culler 1975:205). Such proposal is tantamount to arguing for a poetics of framing – of establishing the borders of a given text's subtexts or elementary units. That endeavor encompasses as well the fundamental – but frequently challenging – mission of determining the beginning and end points of texts embedded within texts. As Bakhtin puts it, 'In order to understand, it is first of all necessary to establish the principal and clear-cut boundaries of the utterance' (*SG*, 112). The same applies when the utterance is extended to encompass an entire text (or subtext).

Crucial to the critical enterprise, analyzing the frame of the text and its constituent narrative components may be understood on several levels. First, it serves in a relatively restricted sense as analogue to the like endeavor of discerning the borders of an utterance constituting a rejoinder in dialogue. Second, in the broader terms of narrative, such effort implies the need to isolate a given subtext from the greater text enveloping it. Finally, it is necessary to establish the bounds of the text itself (generally a given in verbal art). The concept of frame will occupy us here from the linked perspectives of an utterance as 'microtext' and narrative as 'macrotext'. In seeking a fundamental synthesis of this joint concern, the topic will be approached from the frequently complementary viewpoints of the Bakhtin circle and the Moscow–Tartu School of the Semiotics of

Culture, represented here by Yury Lotman and Boris Uspensky, both of whose writings directly engage the problem of frame.[1]

*

Any program of 'framing' seeks to provide definition. For a concept to be meaningful, it must, paradoxically, attain certain limits, meaning that it need not necessarily be limited but *de*limited. It is that kind of attainment that is sought in scholarly endeavor – in the full knowledge that in achieving our goal seeming limitations may also be revealed if the object of research is later assigned even broader dimensions than we had originally conceived. Yet that, too, raises problems of its own. As a case in point, we need only remark Bakhtin's rich concept of dialogism, laid claim to by a vast array of concerns, extending from poetics to politics (which for some is the same).

Framing, for Bakhtin, is related to authoring. An author supplies a necessary set of bounds that are designed to identify a character (socially, psychologically) and establish his place in a fictive world. In creating a separate universe, writ small, the writer isolates an entire life, or complex of lives, within a series of intertwined spatial and temporal planes, which serve to define that universe. This has its analogue, in Bakhtin's thought, in reality as well, where an individual's word is complemented, or responded to, by another's word, framing it in effect, and where a life is also framed by the completing presence of the other. No one can define himself without the helping, healing word of the other; one's life, too, is defined by the presence of another at birth and death, as the temporal bounds of life – and, ideally, during extended moments in between.

In terms of literary narrative and the complex relations inherent to it, 'the interaction between frame and framed is dynamic, and composed of complex "accents and counter-accents"' (Morson 1978:415).[2] As an illustrative instance of such dynamic 'accentuation', when we are asked to take cognizance of 'the "authorial" context surrounding the reported speech' (*MPL*, 118), we are to understand that the reporting context, in effect, frames the reported speech – that the latter is embedded in the former.[3] What is of generic interest in such cases is the interplay between the two. Does the framing authorial context support, reject, or parody what it purports to relate by intonation or other (gestural) means at its disposal? Will the reported speech emerge triumphant or weakened by the manner in which it is framed? These questions, raised by Bakhtin and his fellow theorists, bear heavily on the entire critical enterprise. They are not a reformulation, simply, of the question of point of view. Rather, they ask not only who is speaking at a given moment but whose *ideology* (or world view) is being articulated (or ventriloquated) by the enunciation and – equally important – by the intonation of a set of utterances. Clearly, it may not be the speaker's own viewpoint that emerges as most fully (or sympathetically) developed.

That assessment is made most evident by brief inquiry into the category of quasi-direct speech, which, as a form of reported speech (treated at length by Voloshinov in the monumental study, *Marxism and the Philosophy of Language*), raises perhaps the most engaging questions within the entire Bakhtinian category cataloguing the other person's word. A synthesis of both direct and indirect discourse, it has the potential to combine several points of view. For it is 'precisely a matter of *both* author *and* character speaking at the same time, a matter of a single linguistic construction within which the accents of two differently oriented voices are maintained' (*MPL*, 144). In Uspensky's understanding, quasi-direct discourse combines 'speeches belonging to two different authors: to the speaker himself and to the person about whom he speaks. In other words, we can observe in the author's speech a shifting point of view' (1973:35). That shifting allows for the internal integration of two viewpoints – the mergence of two spheres of speech.

In a fundamental sense, the merging of those spheres implies the integration of two different *texts* belonging to different speakers. We may see just how 'fundamental' by recalling Uspensky's understanding that 'the word *text* has reference to any semantically organized sequence of signs' (ibid.: 5), a typically broad definition of the term affording little range for argument but plenty of room for further delimitation. Each point of view, merged in quasi-direct discourse, has its origins in a certain text: in either the spoken word or what Bakhtin terms 'inner speech'. This gives rise to the potential mergence of several points of view, or set of texts, within quasi-direct discourse. To state that a given point of view originates from a certain text – as the term is defined by Uspensky – correlates essentially with the basic semiotic notions of Bakhtin. However, the latter would more likely prefer to speak of the merging of the speakers' respective ideologies. From Uspensky's perspective, 'text' represents a useful expression when it is still possible to reconstruct and therefore set off reported speech by quotation marks or italics. 'Ideology' might be more suitably employed when there is a greater organic fusion of the two speakers' words. Here the former term is used to highlight the sense of origin of a speaker's point of view, the latter refers to its semantic weight. Bakhtin would say (and Uspensky would likely agree) that you cannot have one without the other: every word, including inner speech, bears its own ideology or particular point of view.

In Uspensky's thought, 'The combination of several points of view is possible not only in a whole work, but also within a single sentence . . .' (ibid.: 34). Bakhtin would amend that to read 'within a single word'. In his view, every discrete utterance contains an expressed ideology. Beyond this, as Uspensky argues, quasi-direct discourse also exists as a social and linguistic strategy that may at times reveal the situational need or convenience for merging the points of view of the speaker and listener, in order to attain an enhanced sense of congeniality or supposed shared sense of viewpoint (an adult speaking with a child, and using a child's mode of speech; a voice of authority attempting a sense of unity with his audience, by employing the first person plural pronoun). In such instances, especially in oral speech, 'the speaker may inadvertently assume the point of view of the person about whom he speaks' (ibid.: 34), allowing for quasi-direct discourse to serve as a social or political ploy for establishing a certain presumed common ground between speaker and listener. In effect, such strategy amounts to an attempt at assailing societal boundaries, a dismantling of the frames that exist as a fundamental part of human interaction.

In the case of the literary work, 'It is as if the author . . . performed the function of an editor reworking the discourse of a particular character' (ibid.: 43). That reworking demands a certain distinguishing sensitivity on the part of the reader, obliged to determine whose voice (or intonation) is most audible at a particular moment in narrative. Perhaps that is the greatest challenge afforded by the technique of quasi-direct speech. In result, the very notion of intonation becomes central – both for Bakhtin, who repeatedly affirms its importance, and Uspensky, who declares that 'while we perceive the feelings of the character from his own point of view, we are constantly listening to the "intonations" of the author' (ibid.: 42), a job that demands acute awareness. For this entails determining where the utterance (or 'text') – with its accompanying ideology – begins and ends, which means, in its most basic (literal) sense, defining its borders, or naming the frame.

In addressing the problem, Bakhtin and his circle argue that linguistics 'is oriented toward the isolated, monologic utterance. Linguistic monuments comprise the material for study, and the passive understanding mind of the philologist is brought to bear on that material. Thus all the work goes on within the bounds of some given utterance. As for the boundaries that demarcate the utterance as a whole entity, they are perceived faintly or sometimes not at all' (*MPL*, 78). In attempting to dispel that latter charge, a distinction is made in *Marxism and the Philosophy of Language* between what are termed 'linear' and 'pictorial' styles in narrative art.

In the former 'a language may strive to forge hard and fast boundaries for reported speech'. The overall intent is 'to demarcate the reported speech as clearly as possible, to screen it from penetration by the author's intonations, and to condense and enhance its individual linguistic characteristics' (*MPL*, 119). This would preclude instances of quasi-direct discourse, the most engaging form of reported speech put forth by this line of thought, where the voice of author and character, or the reporting and reported contexts, appear almost indistinguishable. The charge to the reader and critic is to unravel the two in whatever degree possible. This is likely the most challenging mission assigned the reader by Bakhtin and his fellow theorists: to determine at any given moment just which voice is articulating what ideology. When a text follows the dictates of the linear style, however, that mission is greatly mitigated. 'Here the explicitness and inviolability of the boundaries between authorial and reported speech reach the utmost limits' (*MPL*, 120). The frame, in other words, is clearly and unequivocally delineated, leaving little room for ambiguity.

The pictorial style operates in entirely contrastive manner. In this case, 'Language devises means for infiltrating reported speech with authorial retort and commentary in deft and subtle ways', resulting in two possibilities: either the reporting context will 'resolve' the reported speech within its own expressed, contending ideology; or, the opposite will result.[4] In any event, a certain contention will be expressed verbally or extraverbally (through intonation or gesture) that seeks resolution. However, this is not a straightforward effort. For here the tendency is 'to obliterate the precise, external contours of reported speech' (*MPL*, 120–1), which means, in effect, to mitigate the sense of a distinct frame, as maintained by the juxtaposed linear style. Hence the one affords a clear sense of an expressed ideology (through largely direct discourse), while the other (by means of indirect and quasi-direct speech) relies to a greater degree on the reader to make his own determinations. We may conclude, therefore, that where the linear style is employed, the frames are more clearly delineated, and the reader is less challenged to distinguish between subtle changes in voice and expressed point of view. The pictorial style, on the other hand, by reducing the sense of frame, affords greater subtleties resulting in further corresponding challenges.

Within the context of the pictorial style, a further distinction is effected by the inclusion of a 'texture analyzing modification', whereby instances of direct speech or a clear attempt at retaining the speaker's intonation are maintained within a framework of indirect speech.[5] In this case, 'words and locutions are incorporated in such a way that their specificity, their subjectivity, their typicality are distinctly felt . . .' (*MPL*, 131). Yet their particular specificity is retained to suit the author's needs, so that he can make his point, and emphasize what he wishes to highlight. Mustered, then, in service to the author's purpose, they may be seen in this respect as the speaker's words framed by the author's (or reporting context's) recapitulation or summation. Hence the speaker's selected utterances are framed (as direct speech) by the author's recapitulation of whatever else might have been said (in the form of indirect speech) but deemed not as crucial to his overall purpose.[6] In this 'modification', direct speech is framed by indirect speech, the speaker's words by those of the author, allowing, in effect, for the latter to subvert their original intent or meaning to conform with his own ends. In result, we are afforded a 'verbal envelope' in which the speaker's original expression is retained but where his intention or expressed point of view may not be.

As a closely related, contrastive instance, an additional 'impressionistic modification' is also posited, which is 'used mainly for reporting the internal speech, thoughts, and experiences of a character. It treats the speech to be reported very freely . . . often only highlighting its themes and dominants . . .' (*MPL*, 133). In such instance, authorial intonation is provided, in effect, as an aid to the reader in determining the possible reactions and feelings of a character, resulting in a kind of interpretation of the character's consciousness. Uspensky characterizes a similar case as deriving from 'a potential internal monologue (carried out in the character's own voice), which is then translated into authorial speech' (1973:43). In both modifications, the author's contribution represents an independent text, whose function is interpretive, but appears seamlessly grafted onto the original.

In concentrating on the frame of speech, attention is again called to the 'front line' of the utterance, when it is declared: 'The first and last words, the beginning and end points of real-life utterance – that is what already constitutes the problem of the whole. The process of speech, broadly understood as the process of inner and outer verbal life, goes on continuously. It knows neither beginning nor end. The outwardly actualized utterance is an island rising from the boundless sea of inner speech . . .' (*MPL*, 96). What determines the shape and dimensions of that 'island' are the speaker's linked perceptions of the other and the object of speech. Together they determine how and what he will say. In sum, the boundaries of an utterance are thus determined by both verbal features (since they border on the other person's word) and extra-verbal qualities (since they are dependent upon the referent or object – which may nonetheless be another word or utterance). While both understandings are largely figurative, focusing upon questions of verbal art, our efforts will be grounded in seeking a more concrete perspective.

As a recurring, relatively concrete consideration, the concept of beginning and end bears greatly on the present topic, appearing virtually synonymous with that of frame. As Lotman succinctly puts it: 'The frame of a literary work consists of two elements: the beginning and the end' (1977a:212). However, this formulation may be too succinct, since it does not account for the possibility that within a given work there may also exist a series of frames demarking embedments that denote, for instance, temporal or spatial displacements, situated perhaps within additional such embedments, producing a complex whole – delimited, ultimately, by a beginning and end. Among several engaging functions assigned this paired opposition, Lotman also acknowledges that it serves as a principal organizational factor in a text's basic concern with time and space, both of which issue from 'the categories "beginning" and "end" [which] are the point of departure from which spatial and time constructs can thereafter develop' (1976a:7). What this means, in effect, is that the frame affords the text not only its overt delimitation but its sense of *finiteness* as well. That quality, in turn, allows it, according to this line of thought, to serve as a model of a recognizable world (that is not delimited by a sense of its own finitude). The literary text, in other words, is understood to reflect that world's fundamental ideological views. And it is, in part, its framed aspect that allows it to do so.

In more comprehensive terms, Lotman defines the work of art as 'an area of space demarcated in some way and reflecting in its finitude an infinite object: the world which lies outside the work of art' (1977a:217). The feature which 'demarcates' the work is its frame, understood by Lotman, in its most global sense, as the boundary separating the artistic text from the non-text, the world of the work from the world of man. The relation between the two is dynamic. This is especially important in Bakhtin's thought as well, which heralds the ever-present potential for mutual influence and interorientation. As cited earlier, in his view, 'the real and the represented world . . . are nevertheless indissolubly tied up with each other and find themselves in continual mutual interaction. . . . The work and the world represented in it enter the real world and enrich it, and the real world enters the work and its world as part of the process of its creation . . .' (*DI*, 254). The work of art, from this perspective, may thus be viewed as a dual-directed sign, pointing inwardly to itself as autotelic referent and outwardly to the world which serves as its source of origination, and which it, in turn, models. This modeling capability is realized by virtue of the work deriving from the actual world a series of inherent cultural codes upon which are superimposed a like set of governing generic norms immanent to the world of fiction.

The way such modeling process is effected, in Lotman's view, bears directly on the question of artistic (and non-artistic) space and on the related problem of the frame. 'A work of art is a model of an infinite universe' (Lotman 1977a:210) precisely because it is spatially limited. Lotman takes it as idiomatic that 'a work of art is a finite model of an infinite universe' (ibid.: 210), since the work – in contradistinction to the world – is bounded. Unbounded reality is modeled, according to these lights, by the framed world of the artistic text. 'In modeling an infinite object (reality) by means of a finite text, a work of art substitutes its own space, not for a part (or rather not only for a part), but also for the whole of that reality, the aggregate of all its parts. Each individual text simultaneously models both a particular and a universal object.' Artistic space thus takes on an added crucial dimension in a work beyond affording the sense of a particular place. Employing an already sufficiently burdened expression (but in essential conformity with common usage), Lotman terms that added dimension to a work its 'mythological' quality – 'when the text models an entire universe' – as opposed to its purely 'story' aspect, which 'reflects some episode in reality'. The latter function may be effected by any narrative (a newspaper account, for instance); the former is achieved in myth and by the artistic text. Moreover, Lotman claims that 'it is the mythologizing aspect of a text which is associated primarily with the frame' (ibid.: 211). In making that 'association', he affirms our earlier conclusion that the text, in effect, mirrors a culture's governing ideology or world view. Conversely, the very fact that a text is bounded affords it its modeling capabilities in the first place.

That takes us back to the concept of frame. Significantly, Lotman also posits the possibility of the frame existing as a kind of independent text. In that case, the frame takes on its own importance (as the focus of attention) and special modeling significance. The opening frame in narrative will serve to model the origins of events, the closing frame models ultimate goals. One is ontologically oriented; by showing the beginnings, it demonstrates being. The other is teleologically based, revealing end results. As Lotman puts it, in characteristic telegraphic fashion: 'While the beginning of a text is in some degree associated with modeling the cause, the end activates the feature of the goal' (ibid.: 214). As part of the critical enterprise, then, it must be determined what aspect of the frame predominates. Is the frame to be considered in terms of its being single or dual, open or closed? Examples of the single, open type include epigraphs and the beginning and closing lines of novels. *War and Peace*, for instance, ends on an ellipsis, which makes that novel quintessential instance of a single framed work – left open by definition to further potential realization. Hence 'The end is in principle excluded – the text demands continuation'.

As a further example of this type, Lotman notes the medieval chronicle. 'They are texts which cannot end. If the text is broken off, someone must be found to continue it . . .' (ibid.: 213). Paradoxically, he also regards the chronicle as a classic example of a generic text where the beginning is marked. That medieval form, he argues, exists as well to outline the origins of a given culture, how it all began, why it exists today. It may thus be characterized as bearing a marked beginning, depicting the culture's all-important origins; at the same time it is left open-ended, since, from the perspective of that culture, ideally, it will have no end. Drawing upon that same ideal, an argument may be made for *War and Peace* also modeling, by its inconclusive ending, precisely this ideology.

*

Analogous to the views expressed by the Bakhtin circle, concerning the framing of the utterance, Uspensky concentrates upon the poetics of framing the text.[7] In conformity with Bakhtin's notion of the 'front line' and Lotman's similar emphases, Uspensky likewise affirms the joint concepts of the 'beginning' and 'ending' as having a particular semiotic significance. Constituted by those borders, the frame of the artistic representation is expressed 'in a definite alternation between description structured from within and description structured from without and in the transitions between them' (1973:137). Such structuring permits the work to function, first of all, yet also allows it to be recognized for what it is – a unified system of signs expressing or encapsulating a coherent world view. Conversely, as requisite to perceiving the work as a semiotic system, it is necessary to recognize its borders.

When Uspensky claims that the actual frame of a painting is 'the borderline between the internal world of the representation and the world external to the representation' (ibid.: 143), a similar claim in necessarily figurative terms may be made for reported speech, the other person's word, whose 'internal world' is framed by those words external to it that belong to the reporting context. That analogy is acknowledged by Uspensky, when he states: 'The transition from the external to internal point of view and vice versa may be considered as a natural frame in painting. The same phenomenon may be noted in a literary work' (ibid.: 145). There, of course, he is not speaking literally. However, Uspensky's working definition of 'the phenomenon of framing' implies in his scheme the 'alternation between a point of view internal to the narrative and a point of view external to the narrative' (ibid.: 148), which applies, again, to reported speech. By regarding the alternation between the speaker's point of view and the author's viewpoint (that is, between the reported and reporting contexts), we are able to define the frame or border between the two. Their mutual dependence or 'dynamic interrelation' is defined by the alternation between an 'internal' and 'external' point of view, as noted by Uspensky. Analogous to a tale inserted within a greater encompassing narrative, speech within speech constitutes a relatively discrete unit in the form of direct discourse, or, as quasi-direct speech, appears to 'merge organically with the whole text' (ibid.: 155), creating its own related need for further critical analysis.

Likewise, within verbal art the problem of frame bears on the question of fictions within fiction. As Mukařovský, among others, has pointed out, there is no distinguishing ontological value between truth and lie in fictional texts. Each has its own compositional role to play.[8] Yet there are ample instances of fictive accounts embedded within fiction in clear juxtaposition to 'truthful' tellings of the same or related events. Therefore, accounts of what did not occur within the fictional framework are framed by those events that did 'in fact' take place, raising related questions as to whether they, too, constitute 'discrete units' within a text or are seen to 'merge organically' with it. Generally, within the 'original' (or greater) text, the frame serves in effect to isolate a part of narrative and turn it into a relatively independent text. Uspensky notes that 'the whole narrative text can be sequentially divided into an aggregate of smaller and smaller microtexts, each framed by the alternation of the external and internal authorial positions' (ibid.: 153–4). His concept of 'microtext' again serves handily to establish an analogy from the greater text or narrative to the utterance as the main focus of attention. Indeed, if a text were to be 'sequentially divided', proceeding from one logical subdivision to the next – either thematically or linguistically – the final level of consideration would be the utterance, manifested in its most elementary form as the word, Bakhtin's minimal unit of textual analysis. In Uspensky's scheme, corresponding concepts of 'microtime' and 'microspace' are also assigned to each discrete scene in a work. Such proposal appears to conform, in terms of these basic analytic constituents, with Bakhtin's concept of the chronotope, which claims – at an even deeper level of analysis – for each word in a text its specific locus in time and space.[9]

Further, in relating the literary text and pictorial art as closed semiotic systems, Uspensky declares that each 'presents a unique microworld, organized according to its own laws and characterized by its own spatial and temporal structure'. In more closely linking the two, he states that 'in a literary work and in a work of representational art, a plurality of authorial positions may be present, entering into different kinds of relational patterns' (ibid.: 167–8). Such 'plurality' corresponds to Bakhtin's argument regarding the utterance, whose constant challenge demands that the reader or listener recognize how the 'different kinds of relational patterns' are manifested; that is, determine whose word (and corresponding ideology) is being articulated at any given moment. In recalling Voloshinov's noteworthy dictum, concerning reported speech and the reporting context, which declares that 'dynamic relations of high complexity and tension are in force' (*MPL*, 119), it is just those relations that need to be identified and elaborated in concrete textual analysis. Likewise, similar relations are in evidence between the utterance and the work, between micro- and macrotext, requiring analogous effort at identification and elaboration within their interrelated spheres. Finally, the role and function of the frame itself, manifested in a multiplicity of forms, seeks to elicit its corresponding semiotic determination.

TEXT AND UTTERANCE

From the perspective of the Moscow–Tartu School, the concept of model, or modeling system, is of special significance. An aggregate of characteristic elements comprising an abstract schema, a model sets forth a corresponding set of determinate relations, whose purpose is to enable the analyst to grasp the various kinds of relationships that bind together members of a complex, hierarchically structured organization. In broad terms, it affords a clarifying instance intended to reflect or encapsulate a certain hypothesis regarding some aspect of the world.

According to the common structuralist ploy, a model may be derived from a given binary opposition or series of oppositions. From the School's perspective, and as outlined in its seminal 1973 'Theses', the concept of culture as model may itself 'be regarded as a hierarchy of semiotic systems correlated in pairs . . .' (Lotman *et al.* 1975:76). Providing the key instance of such opposition, culture, according to the School, 'is inseparably linked with the opposition of its "non-culture"', expressed as the contention between the sphere of organization (designed to produce information) in human society and that of disorganization (resulting in entropy) (ibid.: 57, 58). Instances of the former, including myth but especially the artistic text, have since served as the main focus of attention.

In elaborating the importance of the utterance as the basic unit of human communication, Bakhtin distinguishes between primary and secondary utterances. The former are represented by the comparatively simpler mode of everyday speech. Secondary utterances, by contrast, are viewed as literary forms and as more complex – at least in part since a given genre may incorporate features of everyday speech within it, as evidenced especially by dramatic and narrative modes. 'During the process of their formation, they absorb and digest various primary (simple) genres that have taken form in unmediated speech communion. These primary genres are altered and assume a special character when they enter into complex ones' (*SG*, 62). Equated with the notion of the more elaborate secondary utterance, that 'special character' noted by Bakhtin is designated a work of verbal art.

Hence the relatively complex aesthetic mode assimilates the structural principles of the simpler communicative form. In a related, well-known thesis proposed by the Moscow–Tartu School, natural language (as seemingly a more fundamental concept, in the School's parlance, than the utterance, in Bakhtin's) is conceived to serve as the model for all attendant systems of art making. As the primary modeling system, language serves as the model for all other so-called 'secondary modeling systems', by which the members of a culture express themselves (and is, of course, the principal constituent of verbal art). For Bakhtin, on the other hand, the more elemental speech genres are incorporated within – and help determine the making of – complex literary expression. Thus, in both modes of thought, the preeminence of natural language is heralded – but with this distinction: the School proclaims as axiomatic the primacy of language in general as the model for all other modes of cultural expression; Bakhtin focuses upon the spoken language *per se* and its related speech genres as specific sources for the making of verbal art exclusively.

While Bakhtin concentrates upon the utterance as the fundamental unit of analysis in human discourse, the School heralds the text as the exclusive province of the researcher in the study of culture. Exhibiting complementary interests, Bakhtin and the School appear to differ more in emphasis than in substance. The former promotes a new linguistics centered on the utterance as the principle means of human communication, while the latter seeks to establish the semiotics of culture as a discipline founded on the text as the single mode for cultural expression. In evident agreement with the School, Bakhtin declares in his incomplete study on 'The Problem of the Text' that, for the human sciences, 'Regardless of the goals of the research, the only possible point of departure is the text' (*SG*, 104). Bakhtin defines 'text' as 'any coherent complex of signs', yet he also conceives of 'The text as *utterance*' (*SG*, 103, 104). As one criterion for equating text with utterance, he argues that both are individual, unique, and unrepeatable. Significantly, in equating the two, he points to the juncture between his own emphases and those of the School.

However, it is necessary to distinguish between the written utterance *as text* as opposed to the spoken utterance. While Bakhtin clearly distinguishes between speech genres and literary genres, conceiving that the former, simpler mode may indeed be assimilated by the latter, more complex form, he apparently does not question whether they may both be regarded as texts. Rather, he addresses the problem obliquely, when he observes: 'Man in his specific human nature always expresses himself (speaks), that is, he creates a text (if only potential)' (*SG*, 107). On the other hand, the Moscow–Tartu School emphatically makes a clear distinction. In the School's terse, programmatic 'Theses', it is posited that the text be understood as a work that is in some way intentionally *preserved* by representative members of the culture for posterity (Lotman *et al.* 1975:67). Such stricture allows, then, only for the recorded utterance to be regarded as a text and therefore as a possible point of departure for research. According to these lights, Bakhtin's venturesome declaration that 'A human act is a potential text' (*SG*, 107) is an engaging but essentially problematic assertion.[10]

In the jointly held perspective of Bakhtin and the School, the broadly defined concept of the text is understood to be composed of 'sign complexes', which structure all aspects of the text, itself a highly complex sign.[11] This concept may be regarded as analogous on the macrocosmic plane of human culture (comprised of texts) to the word as the basic element composing an utterance on the corresponding microcosmic level of human discourse. Further, in the study of culture, the School posits a hypothetical 'culture text', intended to express the most abstract formulation of a particular culture's 'model of the world' or conception of reality, encompassing, at a projected highest level, a culture's entire production of texts and corresponding ideologies expressed within those texts. No single individual text, in other words, is able to encompass the 'belief system' of a given culture in its entirety; yet each text contributes to an understanding of a collective world view that is refracted through the prism of individual artistic expression.

From the perspective of the School, culture is conceived as 'a mechanism creating an aggregate of texts'; conversely, texts are seen as 'the realization of culture' (Lotman and Uspensky 1978:218). Corresponding to the word in discourse, the text is regarded as the primary manifestation of culture. Or, as otherwise expressed, in seeming agreement with Bakhtin: 'For the study of culture there exists only those messages which are texts. All the others, as it were, do not exist . . . In this sense it may be said that culture is the totality of texts or one complexly constructed text' (Lotman and Piatigorsky 1978:237). Thus the School proposes an all-embracing concept of cultural text, within whose broad domain exist systems that are both non-aesthetic and predominantly aesthetic in orientation, including (among all other art forms) works of verbal art – in which realm, Bakhtin would say, the word is not only the fundamental component but a minimal text itself within that same sphere.

In sum, just as Bakhtin posits the word as the basic constitutive element of the utterance, the School argues that the text is the fundamental significant unit of culture. From this linked perspective, a given text is constituted as a series of utterances, while culture is understood as an aggregate of texts. Each text reflects to some degree the culture in which it is produced; yet no individual text is capable of modeling that culture accurately in all of its many facets. As meaningful fragment, therefore, the text mirrors the greater context of which it is a part in necessarily truncated but potentially significant form.

NOVEL AND CULTURE

The text that will serve as exemplary here is the novel – which, according to Bakhtin's valorizing perspective, is, in its constantly evolving mode, most equipped to reflect upon, or model, the culture in which it is produced. Part of our purpose has been to consider what characteristic features of that kind of text allow for its profound capacity to serve generically as a literary model of a given time and place. That facet of Bakhtin's thinking which comes closest to responding to such question is, as we have seen, his concept of the chronotope – a time/space model that situates the linked temporal and spatial coordinates of every literary image. In the case of the novel, this structuring capability attains additional significance as a result of that genre's basic orientation in the present. From the School's perspective, it might be argued further that the novel as potentially significant social document affirms the School's fundamental notion of culture defined as *memory*. One of the ways in which modern culture 'remembers', in other words, is by means of its most heterogeneous literary mode – the novel.

Centered in the present, Bakhtin conceives of the novel as a temporal model characterized by its immediacy, a heterogeneous, evolving nature, and by a philosophical orientation that likewise remains incomplete and inconclusive. This very indeterminateness, in Bakhtin's view, distinguishes the novel from other genres, affording it a unique potential. Analogous to Bakhtin's concept of the word, the novel's present orientation allows it to refer to a past which is not yet done with, while attempting to take account of a still unknown future destined in turn to be present. In these respects, Bakhtin valorizes the novel's present as an epistemological and axiological pivot, affording an entire range of possibility.

Such argument corresponds with the School's concept of culture and its distinctive ability to continually (re)define itself. Bearing indirectly on the related concept of genre in literary studies, the 'Theses' refer to the 'dynamism of culture', on the one hand, as 'being in principle the fixation of past experience', but which 'may also appear as a program and as instructions for the creation of new texts' (Lotman *et al.* 1975:73). This joint formulation, focusing upon both past and future, correlates with Bakhtin's similar heralding of the role of the novel. But that role, from the School's perspective, is clearly subordinate to the 'dynamism' within a given culture that allows it – by means of the novel and numerous other (artistic) means – to create a 'model of itself, the myth of the culture about itself which appears at a certain stage' (ibid.: 83).

As a form of normative model, Bakhtin claims a special place for the concept of genres as the 'great heroes' of literature and language. But within what Bakhtin himself regards as the special case of the novel, conceived as essentially free of a delimiting canon, the 'hero' of this paradoxical genre must be sought, as has been argued earlier, in the *models* from which the various constitutive modes or forms of the novel derive. Each novel, in other words, is governed by a set of inherently determinate models that are necessarily unique to the given work but which refract at a certain moment in time a particularized view of the culture in which it is produced. As quintessential social document, the novel is thus able to underwrite most consistently a culture's fundamental activity of not only producing texts but of generating a set of texts that function to define the culture itself at its various stages of development. The novel, in effect, may be viewed ideally as affording a multitudinous series of nodal points within a culture's aesthetic sphere, by which the culture perceives and defines itself. Each novel revitalizes the generic concept of the Novel by its very existence as a unique instance within a heterogeneous series of related but frequently very different set of forms. By extension of this definitive function, we may also claim that it reinvigorates a culture's own concept of itself, by affording it a new image, or model, derived from – and reflective of – the given culture.

In *The Structure of the Artistic Text*, Lotman conceives of verbal art in general in much the same *mimetic* terms, when he observes that 'The artist's idea is realized in his model of reality. . . . the artistic message creates an artistic model of some concrete phenomenon; artistic language models the universe' (1977a:11, 18). At a later stage in the same work, he observes: 'A work of art is a finite model of an infinite universe. . . . a work of art is in principle a reflection of the infinite in the finite. . . . It is the reflection of one reality in another . . .' (ibid.: 210). From these linked perspectives we may understand a model to be an 'analogue of reality' (ibid.: 60), which man employs in the process of cognition and in the making of art.

In reflecting upon the mimetic function of art, such argument corresponds with what we have heard from Bakhtin. In addition, the latter explicitly affirms the dual-directedness of the process: not only does the work mirror the world but 'the real world enters the work and its world as part of the process of its creation' (*DI*, 254). This bears directly on the writings of Lotman and Uspensky (1984, 1985), whose works attempt to establish on related principles a viable semiotics of behavior. Taking as their starting point the assumption that the cultural codes of everyday behavior determine in part the making of art, they claim, in a series of related instances, that the aesthetic codes of the artistic work at times determine everyday behavior.

In acknowledging the profound interconnections between literature and life, Lotman makes the striking observation: 'Indeed, the emergence of plot as a definite category that organizes narrative texts in art may in the final analysis be explained by the need to choose a behavior strategy in extra-literary activity' (1984:245). In other words, what remains for the most part an unstructured and perhaps unfulfilled aspect of life – the psychological need to organize our reality according to certain clearly demarcated principles – is realized in the making and formulating of artistic works, narrative texts especially.

Conversely, one may also choose to emulate a behavioral pattern or strategy based on literary models. What begins as an effort to elaborate in fiction the ideological purview of a given culture may thus emerge as a mimetic form of behavior in everyday life. Culture, from this perspective, may thus be envisioned as a hall of mirrors in which literary and personal acts of 'mimesis' are endlessly achieved.

As this era's most representative narrative text (from Bakhtin's perspective), the novel is constituted by plot that is seen as *'a formula of ideologically refracted life'* (Medvedev, *BSP*, 76) – but a 'formula' composed exclusively of variables that leave it essentially undefined. As noted, individual instances of the novel repeatedly and insistently extend its generic 'bounds', leaving it, so far, boundless. So, Bakhtin argues, in the absence of a clearly defined set of norms, and in contrast to all other genres, the novel emerges as a self-revivifying genre through the proliferation of further individual texts that extend its sphere.

The same such claims are applicable to the School's concept of the self-generating mechanism of culture, which, similarly, is potentially unbounded, opposed to all that is deemed non-culture, and is also self-revivifying as a result of its further text production. In fact, the School makes a case for an 'imperialist' tendency in culture that far exceeds the 'expansionist' activity that Bakhtin ascribes to the novel: 'culture, by extending its limits, seeks completely to usurp the whole of extracultural space, to assimilate it to itself . . .' (Lotman *et al.* 1975:59). That same procedure works in reverse, however, resulting in an ongoing struggle between an 'inner' and 'outer' sphere, with each making 'continual breaches in the opposite direction' (ibid.: 61). Such 'breaches' within the realm of novel-making would likely be termed 'innovation'.

In his discussion of the novel, we have seen that Bakhtin consistently privileges openness over closure by favoring a 'centrifugal' as opposed to a 'centripetal' orientation. While the latter attempts to close down the text through reductivist thought, the former seeks further dialogical engagement. Similarly, Bakhtin posits a distinction between what is 'given', or established, and what is 'conceived', or still in process. One is completed and forever closed to further creative development, the other allows for greater differentiation and change.

In like spirit, the School conceives of culture as similarly 'unfinished', and subject as well to a virtually unlimited potential for change. Borrowing further from Bakhtin's terminology, culture, from the School's perspective, may also be viewed as 'conceived', rather than 'given', as a collectively creative event that is still in process. As long as a collective continues to create texts, in other words, the culture will thrive in the self-sustaining process of further self-definition. For a culture to make texts is equivalent to its continued attempt both to define itself and, paradoxically, extend its artistic and ideological bounds. In result of that extension, requiring further effort at self-definition, this vital process continues indefinitely.

Culture, moreover, is viewed by the School as a mechanism whose dynamics might also be described in terms of the consistent opposition between centrifugal and centripetal forces, where the former continually attempts to incorporate additional territories within a culture's given sphere, while the latter represents a disintegrative or reductive force that strives to diminish (from within) that same sphere. In short, the meta-language applied by Bakhtin to the novel appears congruent with the School's general conception of the dynamics of culture, expressed thus:

> The mechanism of culture is a system which transforms the outer sphere into the inner one: disorganization into organization . . . entropy into information. By virtue of the fact that culture lives not only by the opposition of the outer and the inner spheres but also by moving from one sphere to the other, it does not only struggle against the outer 'chaos' but has need of it as well; it does not only destroy it but continually creates it. (Ibid.: 58)

The sense of a similar creative tension is also explored by Bakhtin in regard to the novel. Originating from the constant struggle between centripetal and centrifugal forces, such tension is evidenced in the general opposition between a presumably dominant literary language and mutually contending extraliterary languages that are striving to move from the domain of everyday usage to that of narrative art. The struggle between the one centralizing impulse and other decentralizing tendencies is underscored by Bakhtin's use of the term 'heteroglossia', which succinctly points to such (creative) linguistic contention, seeking dynamic integration, rather than static stabilization.

This same dynamic applies to the interrelations among accepted institutions within a given culture and those still seeking acceptance. As expressed in the School's 'Theses':

> From the position of an outside observer, culture will represent not an immobile, synchronically balanced mechanism, but a dichotomous system, the 'work' of which will be realized as the aggression of regularity against the sphere of the unregulated and, in the opposite direction, as the intrusion of the unregulated into the sphere of organization. At different moments of historical development either tendency may prevail. The incorporation into the cultural sphere of texts which have come from outside sometimes proves to be a powerful stimulating factor for cultural development. (Ibid.: 60)

With regard to the incorporation of extraliterary verbal material, the same might be said of the novel.

Further, the linguistic stratification within the novel correlates on the fundamental level of language, as the raw material from which verbal art is made, with Bakhtin's notion of the genre itself as a self-critical, differentiative, and ever-expanding form. As linguistic usage further stratifies and proliferates in various spheres and directions, in other words, so does the novel, which inevitably follows suit. This tendency of the novel to tread the cutting edge of two opposing orientations results in an intentional linguistic diversity that mirrors a culture's like diversity in terms of linguistic and aesthetic choice, and in other (non-aesthetic) spheres as well. The affinity of the actual world for proliferating new and rarefied forms of linguistic expression is thereby acknowledged within the novel's heteroglottic linguistic plane as, what Bakhtin terms (noted previously), 'a *system* of languages that mutually and ideologically interanimate each other' (*DI*, 47).

In the broad sense in which the School employs the term 'language' – encompassing natural language, the languages of science, of conventional signals (such as road signs), as well as other modes employed by secondary modeling systems, including myth and religion (Lotman 1977a:9) – the same understanding may be applied to culture: namely, that it, too, functions as a system of 'languages'. Or, as the School puts it: 'culture is constructed as a hierarchy of semiotic systems' (Lotman *et al.* 1975:61). Expressed in terms more congruent with Bakhtin's idiom, it is claimed that 'The pursuit of heterogeneity of languages is a characteristic feature of culture' (ibid.: 75) – as, one might add, it is with the novel.

The multiform use of language in the actual world and in the world of the novel exhibits fundamental qualities of both a centrifugal and centripetal nature. The one force allows for greater diversity within the genre (as well as in common usage), the other serves to counteract that possibility. Hence, the dialectics of language use precludes the generalized manifestation of the one tendency without the presence of the other, serving as a counterbalance within a (linguistic or aesthetic) system where one predominates at any given moment.

A similar principle of inclusion and exclusion may be noted in the operation of culture – in its acceptance and rejection of certain forms of religious rite, various art forms, and other contending modes of expression. In this respect, the School perceives two mutually opposed mechanisms at work: 'The tendency toward diversity – toward an increase in differently organized semiotic languages, the "polyglotism" of culture' – as opposed to – 'The tendency toward uniformity – the attempt to interpret itself or other cultures as uniform, rigidly organized languages' (ibid.: 82). These two tendencies clearly cohere

with Bakhtin's distinction between centrifugal and centripetal orientations in the novel. Moreover, in their respective lineaments, they correlate, in effect, with the
School's basic opposition between information and entropy, where the former is conceived as oriented outwardly to embrace additional modes of communication,
while the latter is directed inwardly to reduce such activity.

In the case of the novel, finally, the centrifugal is valorized by Bakhtin as the more dynamic, generally dominant
tendency, generating within numerous felicitous instances new forms as further potential models for the
novel. Likewise, in the spirit of the School, essentially the
same valorization might be made with regard to the functioning of culture, wherein the incorporation of new art
forms, for instance, allows for new ways in which the
culture might express and thereby model itself.

*

Fundamental to this broad notion of contrapuntal juxtaposition, where one generative force counteracts the opposing activity of another, is Bakhtin's equally broad,
seemingly all-encompassing theme of dialogic relations,
which, as the underlying principle of his thinking, is
conceived to embrace all aspects of novelistic structure.
Further, in a more global sense, just as no word or utterance exists in isolation, but is born in response to the
dialogic word of the other, so is each text a responsive text
– both for Bakhtin and for the School. Hence Lotman's
reflection (noted earlier) that texts, as the basic unit of
culture, constitute 'a system of dialogues'.

With regard to what Lotman perceives as 'the presence
in the message of "another's" position', which is fundamental to Bakhtin's concept of the responsive, dialogic
word, the Tartu theorist observes: 'The act of communication is not a simple transmission of a constant message,
but a translation which entails both the surmounting of
sometimes quite considerable difficulties, and specific
losses, and, at the same time, the enrichment of the "I" by

texts bearing another's point of view. As a result the "I" acquires the possibility of becoming "another" with regard to myself' (Lotman 1977c:206–7). That formulation is very close to Bakhtin in both form and substance. As Bakhtin's translator puts it, conveying the spirit of his thought: 'To understand another person at any given moment . . . is to come to terms with meaning on the boundary between one's own and another's language: to translate' (Emerson 1983:24).

By regarding culture as primarily concerned with 'the processing, exchange, and storage of information', Lotman defines culture as a communication mechanism. 'Thus culture is understood as a process and a mechanism characterized by the struggle for information which is received, accumulated, preserved, and coded, decoded and translated from one system into another . . .' (I.P. Winner 1979:106–7). Among these several interrelated considerations, translation is the operative concern. From both Lotman and Bakhtin's perspective, every communicative act implies a corresponding act of translation between the code of the speaker and that of the listener which can only be partially shared at best (since one's use of a given expression may not necessarily correspond with another's understanding of it). Thus, as Lotman affirms: 'those exchanging information use not one common code, but two different ones, to some extent intersecting. Thus the communicative act is not a passive transmission of information but a *translation*, a re-encoding of the message' (1974:302). Communication, then, for both schools of thought, implies *active* translation.

But an act of translation can appear in practice indeed close to that of equation, raising problems of its own. As a case in point, when Bakhtin equates the concept of text with the utterance, which he conceives as being inherently dialogical, it may be supposed that the text also bears an immanent dialogical component. In fact, Bakhtin refers, in an elliptical phrase, to 'The dialogic relationships among texts and within the text' (*SG*, 105). He also makes passing reference to 'a dialogic encounter of two cultures' (*SG*, 7). In such formulations the concept of dialogue appears far

more encompassing than its original concrete usage, raising, at this juncture, the question of whether dialogue
(and its broader derivative, 'dialogism') is to be equated
with intertextuality, or, yet more expansively, with what
may be termed, analogously, 'interculturality'. If so, does
such move from the concrete to the metaphorical strengthen
or weaken Bakhtin's central concept of dialogue, with its
related, fundamental concern for identifying (as accurately
as possible) the speaker, or dominant 'voice' (itself obviously a metaphor), within a given utterance? Moreover,
do we extend our understanding of such terms into the
realm of the figurative at some risk to their general useful-
ness as analytical concepts? Or, would it not be preferable,
after all, to accord dialogue its concrete understanding as
communication between *individuals*? The problem raised
by such questions is whether the concept of dialogism
should be understood to refer not only to informational
but also to both intertextual and intercultural exchange.

7

Dialogic Poetics

Bakhtin was not only a prolific theorist but also a prolific neologist, either coining terms or giving certain expressions a new, greater dimension. Most prominently exemplifying both of these singular aptitudes are his related concepts of dialogism and dialogue respectively. Linguistics, literary theory and other humanistic studies that have appropriated his thought are indebted to Bakhtin for its largesse. But, as part of this heritage, there remains the need to delimit those rich concepts, whose seemingly inexhaustible range of application suggests a debit side as well. What, after all, does dialogism actually mean? When we employ the term 'dialogue', do we use it in its concrete sense or metaphorically? If the latter, then have we extended the idea to the point of such broad application that it becomes entirely overworked or, worse, essentially meaningless?

In the brief two decades during which Bakhtin has emerged from obscurity and exile to world prominence, such concerns have occasioned deserved attention. Yet it is unlikely that the meteoric rise of Bakhtin's star will be matched by a similarly swift resolution of the problematic side of his legacy. Appropriation, it seems, proceeds with greater dynamism and haste than does the more cautionary approach toward delimitation.

Nonetheless, Bakhtin is generally credited with evolving a body of thought that places dialogue squarely in the center. As his cardinal concern, he consistenly maintains that meaning is generated through dialogue, effected by responsive individuals in a potentially endless series of verbal encounters. In response to this insistence upon dialogic relations as the principal source from which meaning is derived, Bakhtin's teachings have been subsumed under the elevated rubric of dialogism. Julia Kristeva, for instance, following a certain intellectual propensity in post-War France, declares that 'dialogism may well become the basis of our time's intellectual structure' (1980:89). But what this might entail and what underlies this seemingly all-inclusive rubric has yet to be clearly defined.

While dialogue may be conveniently juxtaposed to monologue, as a seemingly logical, oppositional concept, such methodological approach appears facile. For the problem of defining monologue is clearly a corollary of the same question initially posed regarding dialogue. Recalling Mukařovský's understanding, monologue results in a single speaker articulating a point of view in the face of another's passivity – that is, silence. However, by not addressing the evident dynamics inherent within such discourse, this viewpoint is clearly inadequate. Silence (itself a possible mode of communication) is, after all, either self-imposed or imposed from without. In either case, the potential for dialogue is significantly reduced.[1] Bakhtin, on the other hand, would say that, in the presence of a (self-proclaimed) authoritative word, the word of the other is intentionally silenced, thus evoking a new, distinctly negative connotation. Representing the distinct counterpoint to this possibility in Bakhtin's humanistic philosophy is the ideologically and radically opposed principle of dialogism, committed to further (potentially unending) ideational exchange.

Intended to accommodate what clearly amounts to the cornerstone of his philosophy, dialogism may be understood to embrace a number of interrelated facets of human discourse. Within its expansive rubric it is designed to account for the participants in dialogue, their inevitable role as ideologues promoting one point of view or another, their similarly inevitable mutual influence upon one another implicit in the degree of persuasiveness brought to their respective arguments, their necessarily differing perceptions of the object of discourse (or referent), and the implicit task of attempting at least partially to reconcile those perceptions. Ultimately, by divorcing the entire concept from the realm of static linguistic generalization, the term is intended to acknowledge the potential for dialogue inherent in discourse. And in so doing, it is meant to bring into clear focus that decisive moment when the word of one speaker actively engages the utterance of another and is itself engaged by that utterance.

How these aspects of dialogical interaction are to be accounted for, and the concept of dialogism understood, may be summarized thus: first, whom one addresses affects, in turn, the manner of address, the speaker's intonation, and the message. Second, the message itself, as previously articulated by both speakers, as well as how it may later be formulated (according to speculative surmise on the part of either speaker), determines the form succeeding messages will take in the ensuing dialogue. Thus, each speaker takes into account what has already been uttered and what may yet be said in formulating any further utterance, allowing for two further mutually exclusive possibilities: either the speaker acknowledges his interlocutor's assessment of things, and may then, in turn, attempt to accommodate that view to his own through a certain 'stylization' of it, or he may attempt to dissuade the other from his stated view, through a perhaps parodic reformulation of it.

In these related respects, the emphasis has been placed on the interlocutors and their respective roles. Yet the material at hand by which dialogue is achieved is the spoken or written word, functioning in a unique manner within an unrepeatable context. As either direct or reported speech, an utterance is contextually determined and therefore wholly distinctive. At the same time it affords an infinite potential for possible concrete instances of dialogue, when the word is free to convey information and a stated point of view. Ideally, meaning is sought and perhaps derived through dialogical interaction on the part of a set of interlocutors. Yet the concept of dialogue has also accrued a figurative dimension that requires brief review.

In an essay titled 'Dialogue and Dialogism', Paul de Man attempts to distinguish between these two key

Bakhtinian concepts, representing a much needed move in that direction. The former term is taken in its common understanding to mean the exchange of information in the form of alternating responsive discourse. Beyond this, as we have seen, dialogue was also taken by Bakhtin to signify what was for him the paramount property of language – its inherent ability to effectuate that responsive exchange. Language exists to make dialogue possible. Conversely, dialogue appears immanent to language. In these linked respects dialogue remains concrete and distinct from dialogism.

The latter term, by contrast, remains less clearly delimited both in de Man's understanding and generally. Its thrust for de Man is in two basic directions. First, the term is deemed metalinguistic, since it 'says something about language rather than about the world. Bakhtin is consistent in his assertion that the dialogical relationship is intra-linguistic, between what he calls two heterogeneous " voices," as in a musical score.' That comprises one property; the other derives logically from the first: 'the function of dialogism is to sustain and think through the radical exteriority or heterogeneity of one voice with regard to any other, including that of the novelist himself' (1983:102). Here the emphasis shifts from language to alterity – the search for and possible recognition of the other. Dialogism thus implies a potential shift from linguistic possibility (including, as de Man holds, the ability to engage in formal methods of analysis) to the possibility of not only recognizing the other but also recognizing his otherness. Thus 'Bakhtin at times conveys the impression that one can accede from dialogism as a metalinguistic (i.e., formal) structure to dialogism as a recognition of exotopy' (that is, the recognition of otherness) (ibid.: 103). That assessment not only appears consonant with the spirit of Bakhtin's usage but also succinctly encapsulates the perhaps most engaging feature of dialogism that has caused its extraordinarily wide appropriation. But this raises problems of its own.

For one thing, as de Man explains: 'In this perspective, dialogism is no longer a formal and descriptive principle, nor does it pertain particularly to language: heteroglossia (multivariedness between discourses) is a special case of exotopy (otherness as such) and the formal study of literary texts becomes important because it leads from intralinguistic to intracultural relationships' (ibid.: 102–3). The latter notion is of interest for the moment. Does it not constitute a certain legerdemain as a peculiar mode of appropriation, by which Bakhtin himself, and virtually every reader since, has assimilated dialogism to mean – finally, above and beyond all else – the study of cultural relations? Because if so (engagingly so), then, as de Man pointedly declares: 'one should perhaps ask who, if anyone, would have reason to find it difficult or even impossible to enlist Bakhtin's version of dialogism among his methodological tools or skills' (ibid.: 104). Hence the ease with which Bakhtin's preeminent concept is accommodated – itself ill- (or too 'openly') defined, thereby encouraging what appears an excessively broad appropriation for which Bakhtin himself is partly accountable.

In his concern to delimit the concept (and therefore its attendant proliferated assimilation), de Man reasonably argues: 'Whether the passage from otherness to the recognition of the other – the passage, in other words, from dialogism to dialogue – can be said to take place in Bakhtin as more than a desire, remains a question for Bakhtin interpretation to consider in the proper critical spirit' (ibid.: 103). His point, well taken, is of interest on two counts: first, he charts the 'passage' from dialogism to dialogue, when one suspects that the motivating force of assimilation (and appropriation) is in the other direction; second, the statement implies a shift from figurative to literal understanding, and by further implication, from intra- and inter-cultural exchange to intra- (Bakhtin's 'inner speech') and inter-personal discourse. This move, in fact, may be what is needed to afford dialogism a definitive concrete meaning beyond (or before) its accrued figurative considerations.

*

When referring to artistic works, aesthetic systems, or entire cultures as 'interacting' or 'influencing' one another, we speak, of course, metaphorically. Only individuals interact. The literary work, regardless of common usage, does not influence other works and is itself not influenced. The same obviously goes for the system (or genre) and culture of which it is a part. Yet each of these manifestations is commonly thought of in terms analogous to their human source. We are therefore inclined to say that texts, genres, and entire cultures are engaged in a kind of 'dialogue'. Currently in vogue, the term 'intertextuality' is essentially derived from such figurative thinking. Moreover, the expressions 'dialogic' and 'intertextual' are frequently treated synonymously. When taken out of the human context, however, the former term clearly reverts to its figurative essence. While this view of dialogism may serve as a descriptive model for expressing the intricacies by which artistic works and aesthetic systems are interrelated, a distinction should nonetheless be observed in that concept's concrete as opposed to metaphorical usage.

This evident distinction bears on the question of how information is supplied and meaning derived. In concrete terms, we may say with Bakhtin that meaning (or some accord approaching mutual understanding) is generated between individuals engaged in dialogue. But that essential schema does not suffice to answer the same question posed with regard to the work of art or other cultural manifestation. Composed of a conventional system of signs employed in *sui generis* fashion, intra- and intertextual relations presuppose a different or necessarily revised set of questions.

In figurative terms, we may say that the dialogic principle is also revealed in the interrelations and interconnections among texts, commonly expressed as intertextuality. Just as no word or utterance may be said to exist in isolation, but is born in response to the dialogic word of the other, so is each text a responsive text. A further related concern, discussed first in Prague and later in Tartu, are the interrelations among the various institutions of culture as a whole, comprising a higher set – to use Bakhtin's metaphor – of dialogic relations. In contrast to the monologic, putatively authoritative, single-voiced utterance, which closes off the possibility of further discourse, dialogic activity is understood as 'a questioning, provoking, answering, objecting activity' (*PDP*, 285) that allows for the process – whether on the interconnected planes of the quotidian, (inter)textual, or cultural – to go on endlessly.

As Bakhtin puts it, proclaiming the extensive range of his subject, 'dialogic relationships are a much broader phenomenon than mere rejoinders in a dialogue . . . they are an almost universal phenomenon, permeating all human speech and all relationships and manifestations of human life – in general everything that has meaning and significance' (*PDP*, 40). In approaching this all-encompassing notion, two features emerge as especially prominent: its universal claim and its implicit figurative formulation. Only human beings (and perhaps some other creatures) engage, after all, in dialogue – not languages, texts, or cultural institutions. Nonetheless, the metaphorical aspect appears to legitimate (but not, of course, substantiate) the universal. If the concept is therefore to be reconciled with its author's grand intentions, it will require a more clearly defined substantive meaning.

Inherent within human dialogue, its participants utilize a certain well-established semiotic system (a natural language accompanied by attendant intonational and gestural patterns), allowing for the possibility of extended or renewed clarification and interpretation of possibly differing views. The literary text, by contrast, is conclusively encoded as a system of signs delimited almost entirely by natural language (situated by a system of punctuation and typographical arrangement) that at a certain critical moment (within the publishing process) does not normally afford the possibility for emendation or change. In the one case the participants actively *utilize* a system of conceivably 'renewable' signs, in the other the text is *composed* of essentially unalterable signs. The encoding process of the one remains open to 'revision' so long as the speakers are available to one another. In the case of the finished text, however, no such possibilities for further encoding exist, although the potential for an infinitely variable, rich and contending, decoding procedure remains open to new understandings brought to bear by cultural and historical, as well as personal, experience.

These rather simplistic distinctions nevertheless bear critically on the differences between concrete and figurative understandings of dialogue. For at this juncture the one concrete dialogic situation is clearly not coincident with its figurative 'dialogic' counterpart. The one appears less definitive and more flexible regarding the encoding procedure, the other offers greater possibility at the level of decoding as a result of an inherent ambiguity and desired complexity. This undestanding allows for the further development of what Thomas Winner refers to as 'semiotic inter-art and intra-art comparative studies' (1978:229), still in their respective nascent stages. If the concept of dialogism is to be applied and extended beyond human discourse to the realm of cultural artifacts (and their interrelations), as has commonly occurred, a corresponding concrete set of temporal and spatial, as well as ideological, relations among elements constituting a single work, on the one hand, and among works constituting a given culture, on the other, must be designated. How such constitutive elements of a text function and are integrated within it are problems analogous to the question of how a work is related to other works and to the culture of which it is a part. This also applies to the manner in which the elements of a text designate a specific referent as well as how the component texts within culture likewise make reference to the world.

Clearly different is that concept of dialogue, understood as the concrete exchange of verbal utterances between two or more interlocutors, as opposed to an understanding that situates the expression at the intersection of intra- as well as intertextual relations. In this respect, the term – with its implications for literary theory – is clearly burdened. To extend the point, the same problem also applies to the concerns of cultural semiotics. Mukařovský speaks of the interrelations among the institutions of literature, law, religion and economics – but he does not slip into the pitfall of regarding cultural operations as being encompassed under the rubric of the grand workings of dialogism or some other figurative force. Are we, then, doing this in his – or Bakhtin's – stead? In other words, once we depart from a relatively clearly defined understanding of dialogue, and proceed into the murkier, figurative realm of dialogism, do we not burden the concept too greatly, so as to come up with less, when we thought we had more?

Nonetheless, to relegate figurative understanding to the periphery of meaning would be both literal minded and counterproductive, glossing over nuances in the process that are essentially fluid. A clearly delineated 'boundary' (itself a generic consideration to which Bakhtin is especially sensitive) between concrete and figurative concerns is likely to appear only partially distinguishable at best. The problem of intonation, with which Bakhtin was prominently concerned, may serve as a case in point. We read that 'the basic elements constituting the form of the utterance are *first of all* [italics added here] the *expressive sound* of the word, its intonation, then the *choice* of words and, finally, their *arrangement* in the whole utterance' (Voloshinov, *BSP*, 126). Primary emphasis is thus placed on the role of intonation in the formation of an utterance. Further, it is claimed that 'Intonation plays the most essential part in the construction of the real-life and of the literary utterance too'. If such were the case, however, there is a sure blurring of distinction. In 'real-life' discourse intonation is correctly understood in concrete terms (we do after all intone our words purposefully while speaking); however, intonation in the literary utterance can only be conceived figuratively (unless we understand it to be composed, or read, aloud).[2] This is so because although intonation is seen as 'the most flexible and the most sensitive transmitter of social relations', it is nevertheless '*the expression in sound of a social evaluation*' (Voloshinov, *BSP*, 127). Sound, here, is the crucial point.

One way to hold the rich theoretical concept of dialogism

to meaningful practical endeavor is to apply it to the critical enterprise of examining the writer's use of language – or languages, as Bakhtin would have it. This concern has been underscored in his discussion of heteroglossia, whose charge is to account for the inherent interaction among a multitude of possible *words* in narrative. In attempting to render such account, we are challenged to discern whether more than one 'voice' may be registered at any given moment and whose voice it is.[3] The concern with voice, which amounts to a concern with ideology, is surely one of the most rewarding critical pathways Bakhtin's thought has illuminated for us. For to determine voice is to reveal authorship – and with it, a concomitant ideology that may be expressed and, in turn, apprehended, in a single utterance exclusively or in an entire text.

Just as it is critical to acknowledge how individuals engaged in dialogue relate to one another, their verbal material, and to their world (or some chosen referent within it), so must the relations among corresponding elements and their particular referents within a single work of art, or the ties among several interrelated works, be clearly designated. Otherwise, for better or worse, our understanding of dialogism on the level of a single text or entire culture remains essentially a figurative concept, in contrast to what Bakhtin terms in one felicitous stroke: 'Real dialogue (daily conversation, scientific discussion, political debate, and so forth') (*SG*, 124). It is in this latter case that we find the potential whereby it may be justly claimed that, 'Every thought and every life merges in the open-ended dialogue' (*PDP*, 293), allowing for the ideal to become real.

*

Yet that 'ideal', as another perceived form of dialogism, has its challengers as well. In brief summary, the challenge to Bakhtin centers precisely on those widely appealing positive, spiritual, healing qualities that have been both implicitly and explicitly attributed to dialogism by

Bakhtin himself and his readers. As Caryl Emerson poses the problem: Bakhtin 'seems to assume that dialogue just naturally optimizes itself for its participants. Is it not equally plausible', she asks, 'that making dialogue happen takes a lot of inner work, work that is not social in its essence but more like moving rocks in a field you want to plow, or a struggle against terror?' Further, Bakhtin's 'benevolence', as she terms the presumption of benignness that is characteristic, in her view, of Bakhtin's thought, 'is the most appealing and perhaps the most troublesome aspect of his poetics' (1988:514, 517).

That aspect is taken up in various engaging ways by current readers of Bakhtin who further question that 'benevolence', particularly in light of twentieth-century experience. Thus, Aaron Fogel argues that 'communication itself is by nature more coercive and disproportionate than we think when we sentimentalize terms like *dialogue* and *communication*' (1989:195). That observation questions whether Bakhtin himself and his perhaps too zealous readers have not overlooked certain potentially negative features that also figure at times as part of human dialogue. Can dialogism deliver all that it seems to promise? Are not certain basic (nasty) features of human nature being overlooked? Like physically coerced speech (including torture), a common feature especially of twentieth-century reality that is well-documented both in literature and by oral account – of which Bakhtin could not possibly have been ignorant on either count.

In concentrating upon the problem of coerced speech, Fogel explores the idea that 'all dialogue, even dialogue with the self, involves coercive disproportion', allowing, in the struggle for dominance, for one speaker perhaps to have a far greater say than another. Moreover, as an attendant item that Bakhtin chose to ignore, we are reminded that 'forced dialogue' (ibid.: 180, 184) is likewise a common event, whereby an individual actively seeks to *make* another speak. That effort may take at least two forms: the extortion of information for some kind of political use or the persistent seeking after a certain supposed 'truth' – which in the end may, ironically, destroy the seeker.

Such readings, in effect, take up the issue of Bakhtin's being too soft in expounding his dialogical principle in light of the ever present harshness of human reality. Taking a stronger view that emphasizes 'the provocation of the word by the word', the argument is put forth that a greater range in chronicling much that is disturbing in twentieth-century experience is needed beyond what Bakhtin proposes. Further, in this line of thought it is maintained that 'coercion to speak, the will to make the other speak . . . is the pattern of most (if not all) dialogue relations' (ibid.: 189). In this dim view 'forced dialogue' appears the norm. Beginning with the relatively benign observation that someone must initiate dialogue for dialogue to ensue, we are enjoined more thoroughly to explore *how* that dialogue is initiated. Is it accomplished by generally peaceful means or by more subtly coercive, even brutal efforts? The question fairly demands response.

That argument, in its generality, outlines significantly an *attitude* toward dialogue that Bakhtin did not explore – one that is not just simply 'monologic' (that is, insistent upon its own authority) but aggresive, even violent. In fact, Bakhtin did recognize that monologism may possibly erupt in violence, that it may even have its source there. He did not, however, explore aggressive modes of achieving dialogue. Yet such 'omission' of itself detracts little from Bakhtin's argument. That violence exists as a possible mode of human interaction remains a fact – with or without Bakhtin's (unlikely) sanction, with or without the critic's prolonged attention. What is achieved, nonetheless, is to explore another – albeit regrettable – dimension of dialogue, expanding the bounds by which it may be conceived, without necessarily reducing or limiting Bakhtin's positive view regarding its potential. In arguing this case, the compelling point is made that 'If there is to be "dialogue," someone must make it happen. This idea . . . rejects definition of "dialogue" or "communication" as simple interpersonal freedom, or as something inherently "mutual," "sympathetic," or "good"'. From the critic's perspective, 'We are on the verge of an idea of dialogue that is in fact unexpected and difficult to identify comfortably; on the one hand this idea seems potentially authoritarian and on the other intellectually freeing' (ibid.: 193–4). In what way remains to be seen.

From another related perspective that likewise challenges Bakhtin, this juxtaposed, unsmiling aspect of dialogue may simply appear as the other side of this all too *human* Janus face. Man, after all, must deal with himself, with time, with the fact that it is virtually impossible to utter a 'new' word (in Bakhtin's understanding), given that we are all but mired in the utterances of others, who have ineluctably penetrated our hopefully original words with their own. All this takes its toll – and is necessarily reflected, as part of the human condition, in literature.

In making this case, Michael André Bernstein strikes a chord similar to what we have just heard. 'Instead of the generous mutual attentiveness that a dialogue is supposed to foster, what we find just as often are speakers stalking one another with the edgy wariness of fighters ready to erupt into lethal violence the moment one of them senses an opening.' Thus, for this reader of Bakhtin as well, 'the very dialogism [Bakhtin] celebrates already contains a darker and more desperate strand than his account usually acknowledges' (1989:199, 204). Why 'already'? Because man may suffer, as Dostoevsky makes abundantly clear in *Notes From Underground*, an excess of remembrance, the sort of recollection that causes unbounded grief, resentment, and impotence, from which there is no escape (since, in part, the subject does not want to), offering at the very best only marginal resolution. At the center, then, is memory – 'already' present at any given moment. In the extreme instance chronicled by Dostoevsky, as the case in point, 'A maddening sense of impotence is united to a daemonicaly obsessive total recall, until the sufferer's entire consciousness is like an open sore whose sight evokes only disgust in both the victim himself and those around him' (ibid.: 205). This, too, represents a strong divergence from Bakhtin's call for 'healthy' immersion in mutually soul-saving activity – drawn this time, no less, from the very center of Bakhtin's own intellectual sphere.

In result, in *Notes*, the character is locked into an unending dialogue (with invisible interlocutors), in which at least part of his inner torture is centered in the clear realization that not a single utterance of his is original. His prison house of language, in this case, is a prison house of previous utterances, to which his responses are likewise old hat. Nothing Dostoevsky's tortured consciousness has to say has the ring of originality even for the speaker himself. That is what makes it so awful, causing the speaker to go on relentlessly. The task set here is to 'consider the bitterness with which even the most worldly characters respond to a feeling of imprisonment in dialogues they know consist only of citations from earlier dialogues' (ibid.: 211). The problem is a profound one. In such instances, dialogism is not simply a literary technique by which the story unfolds, but constitutes instead the paramount problem with which the character must contend: in short, the unholy mesh that emerges from an obsessive self immersed in what Bakhtin valorizes as the word of the other evoking a responsive word from the self. Accented thus, this self-repelling version of the dialogic principle appears both abhorrent and inescapable to the character engaged in such 'exchange'. Hence 'dialogism itself is not always just clement or life enhancing . . . the resonance of multiple voices may be a catastrophic threat as much as a sustaining chorale' (ibid.: 199).

Part of the problematic, expressed darkly in this view, is present in the well-known formulation, which defines reported speech as 'speech within speech, utterance within utterance, and at the same time also *speech about speech, utterance about utterance*' (*MPL*, 115), and which highlights one of the most rewarding and challenging paths for further study of dialogic discourse. Here the critic explores in concrete terms what had been theoretically charted. But where Bakhtin had projected promise he finds menace; the word of the other may indeed afford further insight into the self, but what monstrous image may not emerge from such confrontation?

Beyond this lurking possibility, moreover, there lies in wait yet another problematic of monstrous proportion –

the issue of time. No one escapes it, our lives are defined by it. But few are condemned to live a life inordinately governed by the dictates of the past. This specter also figures as part of the argument. Part, after all, of being mired in quotation – in one's own and the previous utterances of others – amounts to being unduly engaged by the past. The result, in paraphrase of Nietzsche, is 'the fundamental nature of revenge as a constant and nagging rage at the human experience of temporality' (ibid.: 214). That rage in creative narrative form, furthermore, may be wide ranging: 'it is the peculiar logic joining fiction, dialogism, and temporality as mutually linked sources of *ressentiment* that determines the narrative structure of exemplary texts like *Notes from Underground* and constitutes one of the central imaginative crises of nineteenth-century thought. Freudian neuroses may be specific and personal, but *ressentiment* is, by definition a herd phenomenon: the state of mind, temperament, and imagination of a being who suffers most from the realization that even his worst grievances lack any trace of particularity' (ibid.: 213).

If such is indeed a universal case, then this argument takes us full circle. As noted at the outset, Bakhtin argues against a mode of thought, which he terms 'theoretism', as a form of reasoning that abrogates the individual in favor of the general. Hence, in those cases where 'reminiscence-as-suffering operates as a kind of master trope' (ibid.: 204), the resultant literary form, with its particular (suffering) character type, represents in narrative what Bakhtin argues in theory: that man, as Dostoevsky also well knew, cannot afford on any account to give up his personal quest for meaning in acquiescence to an understanding that belongs to the mass. No matter the cost.

Notes

Portions of this book have been published in earlier versions that have since been substantially revised. They include: 'M.M. Bakhtin's Concept of the Word', in *American Journal of Semiotics* (1984), 3 (1), 79–97; 'Word, Utterance, Text', in *Semiotica* (1988), 72 (1/2), 179–86; 'Dialogism: Perspectives and Delimitations', in *Canadian–American Slavic Studies* (1988), 22 (1–4), 43–50; 'Bakhtin and Lotman: Novel and Culture', in *Semiotics of Culture*, eds Henri Broms and Rebecca Kaufman (Helsinki: Arator Inc., 1988), 233–44; 'Sign and Spirit: The Semiotics of M.M. Bakhtin', in *The Semiotic Web 1988*, eds Thomas A. Sebeok and Jean Umiker Sebeok (Berlin, New York: Mouton de Gruyter, 1989), 17–40; 'The Concept of Frame', *Working Papers and Pre-Publications*, Centro Internazionale di Semiotica e di Linguistica, Universita di Urbino, Number 189, December 1989; 'The Legacy of M.M. Bakhtin', in *Semiotica* (1991), 83 (1/2).

1 Bakhtin and His Circle

1. All references to works produced by Bakhtin, as well as by members of his 'circle', including V.N. Voloshinov and P.N. Medvedev, will be abbreviated in the text, as indicated in the Bibliography under primary sources.
2. Existing in varying stages of completion, these essays have been published in English under the title, *Speech Genres and Other Late Essays*.
3. For the most fully developed account to date of Bakhtin's life and intellectual milieu, see Clark and Holquist's excellent study *Mikhail Bakhtin*, to which the present abbreviated survey of these concerns is indebted.
4. The essential points of the authorship dispute, as well as how the entire argument lines up, may be followed by examining these positions, most prominently representing the two points of view: Titunik (1976); Clark and Holquist (1984:146–70); Morson (1986); Titunik (1986); Clark and Holquist (1986); Morson and Emerson (1989:31–49). In sum, the dispute centers on the question of whether to retain the original putative authorial credit until such time (should that ever occur) that the matter receives a definitive resolution, indicating a need for change. In this respect, the question need occupy us no further here, nor intrude upon the subsequent discussion of the ideas themselves, deserving consideration, and elaborated in a succession of works, no less remarkable for their having been written (entirely or partly) by one or another of these fortuitously rediscovered thinkers. When works belonging to the other

two theorists are cited in support of Bakhtin's thought, those citations are indeed considered ones: their voices, in these instances,
are meant to complement his. It is therefore supposed that no
injustice will have been perpetrated in an area requiring judicious-
ness and sensitivity.

5. As a current member of the Moscow–Tartu School affirms: 'dialogue
is unquestionably the dominant of [Bakhtin's] scientific creativity,
the central and key concept around which his principal themes and
achievements are grouped' (Ivanov 1974:321). And, as an *émigré*
member of the School corroborates: 'All the main themes, discover-
ies and achievements for which philology now gives credit to Bakhtin are crystallized around this central notion' (Segal 1974:128). This
joint assessment is reaffirmed by Bakhtin's biographer, who asserts
that Bakhtin's work 'may be summed up as dialogism, since the
particular way Bakhtin models the relation of self and other is a
dialogue of a special kind' (Holquist 1983:308).

6. This is paradoxical in a sense, since Bakhtin categorically rejects
semiotics, in his 'Notes of 1970–71', as dealing with the 'transmission of ready-made communication using a ready-made code'
(*SG*, 147). That terse isolated understanding regards the doctrine of
signs, with its emphasis on the generalized concept of code, as
approaching the kind of thinking which Bakhtin rejects as 'theoretism'. Nonetheless, too much, it seems, has been made of a single
line – devoid of a larger context – within a whole corpus of writing.

7. In a recent assessment, reiterating previous acknowledgements,
Igor Chernov, a younger member of the School, states unequivocally in an historical overview that the figure of Bakhtin and his
ideas 'fortified' the School (1988:16).

8. Bakhtin, in principle, eschews binary thinking, which he associates
with structuralism, in his view, a fruitless mode of approach. However, in practice, we regularly encounter such paired oppositions,
beginning with the implied juxtaposition of monologue and dialogue, the positing of 'centrifugal' as opposed to 'centripetal' forces,
framed versus unframed, what is 'given' juxtaposed to what is
'conceived' – all serving as immediately recognizable hallmarks of
his thought (to be discussed later). These cannot be explained away,
yet might be viewed as perhaps universally typical strategies for
philosophical argumentation that Bakhtin might 'eschew' but could
not entirely avoid.

9. A single expletive uttered by a President, for instance, may well be
treated as an entire text, endlessly discussed.

2 The Word

1. Whether that formulation and attendant borrowing represents a
valid extension of Bakhtin's thought in the direction of semiotics, or
a derailing in direct contradiction of his views, will likely prove a
matter of ongoing debate. The position taken here favors the former

understanding. For a differing viewpoint, see Morson and Emerson (1989:30).

2. In *Marxism and the Philosophy of Language* a distinction is made between 'meaning' and 'theme'. The latter refers to 'the contextual meaning of a given word within the conditions of a concrete utterance', while the former implies 'the meaning of a word in the system of language or, in other words, investigation of a dictionary word' (*MPL*, 102). Such distinction makes possible (if not completely viable) the following formulation: 'Meaning, in essence, means nothing; it only possesses potentiality – the possibility of having a meaning within a concrete theme' (*MPL*, 101). Thus the word is liberated both from the dictionary and from its 'meaning' when it is utilized in a given context, which allows it to function as a 'theme' bearing its own highly defined, particularized sense. The 'ideological sign par excellence' is thus destined to lead the 'true life of the word' only through the sustained social interaction of its users. Conversely, no word exists – or has meaning – devoid of context.

3. Both *The Formal Method in Literary Scholarship* and *Marxism and the Philosophy of Language* are devoted in large part to articulating the social quality of the word. In the former, it is claimed that the word attains the vitality of 'a living thing' through what is termed 'social evaluation', by which the utterance is actualized 'both from the standpoint of its factual presence and the standpoint of its semantic meaning'. In giving it meaning, then, 'Social evaluation is needed to turn a grammatical possibility into a concrete fact of speech reality' (*FM*, 121, 123). In the latter work, we read that 'the reality of the word, as is true of any sign, resides between individuals. . . . The sign is a creation between individuals, a creation within a social milieu' (*MPL*, 14, 22). While retaining the material sense of the word, such assertions also affirm its social significance – the fact that it bears meaning only in the verbal interaction or dialogue among its users.

4. The written text is conceived in similar terms: 'every literary work *faces outward away from itself*, toward the listener–reader, and to a certain extent thus anticipates possible reactions to itself' (*DI*, 257). With regard to the 'written utterance', moreover, a case is made for its also being dialogical in nature; for aside from the possibility of its being a chosen topic in dialogue, a book – that is, '*a verbal performance in print* . . . is calculated for active perception, involving attentive reading and inner responsiveness, and for organized, *printed* reaction in various forms . . .' (*MPL*, 95). This point will later be taken up in greater detail.

3 The Novel

1. As a case in point, Bakhtin's chronotopic model illustrates such 'dual-directed' relations, since it is concerned both with how a given text comes into being at a certain time and place, and with how that

text might be interpreted as a result of those same determining cultural factors that produced it in the first place.

2. For an expanded discussion of the possible relations among temporal aspects of the novel, see Danow 1986.

4 Self and Other

1. The idea is positively expressed thus: 'The word, the living word, inseparably linked with dialogic communion, by its very nature wants to be heard and answered' (*PDP*, 300). And further: 'the word, which always wants to be *heard*, always seeks responsive understanding . . .' Conversely, its corresponding negative formulation, expressing the sad result of a steadfast (monologic) resistance to dialogue, appears both poignant and condemning: 'For the word (and, consequently, for a human being) there is nothing more terrible than a *lack of response*' (*SG*, 127).

2. The other two templates are direct and indirect discourse. The topic of reported speech will be taken up later in greater detail.

5 The Prague School

1. The notion of a 'dialectical antinomy' is applied by Mukařovský to the interaction between the two functions in a given work, between aesthetic and extra-aesthetic areas, and between artistic and non-artistic phenomena in a given culture (see Veltruský 1981:139, 141–2). Concerning the artistic work, Mukařovský posits the notion of a 'semantic gesture' or semantic intention, by which the poet 'unifies the contradictions, or "antinomies," on which the semantic structure of the work is based' (Mukařovský 1978:110).

2. Likewise, it is rightly observed: 'the structure of the work of art is part of the intentionality of both creator and perceiver. Mukařovský compares the evolution of the arts to an uninterrupted *dialogue* between encoders and decoders, between all those who successively create, and all those who successively perceive, art' (Winner 1976:447; italics added).

3. A further development of this point of view reads as follows: 'Bakhtin's idea was to find a *new* minimal unit of social analysis . . . from which both the social and individual, the macro- and micro-, the systematic and the unsystematic could be derived. . . . In [this] case, "minimal unit" refers to a unit of analysis that retains all the basic properties of the whole and which cannot be subdivided further without losing those properties. . . . The double-voiced word, the dialogic utterance, would be such a unit and could form the basis for the general science of culture and for its constituent disciplines' (Morson 1983:231–2).

6 The Moscow–Tartu School

1. In effect, our present concern represents an elaboration of the following astute remark: 'The early formalists saw the embedded narrative and play with *the framing of stories by stories* as a model of narratology; Baxtin and Voloshinov attribute analogous significance to the embedded speech act' (Morson 1978:414). The purpose here is to attempt to establish a series of connections between these two spheres.

2. Or, as Voloshinov puts it: 'Between the reported speech and the reporting context, dynamic relations of high complexity and tension are in force' (1973:119).

3. In Voloshinov's terminology, 'author' may retain its common meaning but also signifies the one who reports another's speech. Hence 'authorial' is used synonymously with 'reporting speech', as that context surrounding reported speech. The dynamism noted between reporting and reported speech (fn.2 above) is therefore equivalent to that between authorial and reported speech.

   Uspensky also uses 'author' in the common sense of 'the person to whom belongs the whole text that we are examining', but also equates 'authorial' speech with 'one's own' speech as opposed to 'someone else's' speech, following Voloshinov (1973:33).

4. Uspensky expresses in relatively simple terms the same two possibilities: either there will be felt 'the influence of someone else's speech on authorial speech', or there will be exercised 'the influence of authorial speech on someone else's speech' (1973:33, 41).

5. Italics, use of quotation marks, and other conventional notations that set off a passage from surrounding material represent additional instances of embedment, deserving attention as peripheral topics within the present discussion.

   The emergence of direct discourse from within indirect speech is described by Voloshinov in a handsome metaphor as being 'like those sculptures of Rodin's, in which the figure is left only partially emerged from stone' (1973:132).

6. Examples of this form are common in trial and investigation scenes, as in the concluding chapters of *The Brothers Karamazov*.

7. In addition to verbal art, Uspensky also discusses pictorial art and the related concept of the frame in its concrete sense. Both of these aspects of his discussion fall outside the bounds of the present one.

   Aside from the actual frame in pictorial art, Uspensky treats the frame as 'a special compositional form which structures the representation and invests it with symbolic meaning . . .' (1973:140), setting off the work, or a part of it, as a separate semiotic sphere or artistic world bearing its own individual meaning.

8. Hence 'The fact of whether, to what degree and in what manner the writer presents the narrated event as real or fictional, will be . . . an important element of the structure of the literary work . . .' (Mukařovský 1970:73).

9. Nonetheless, Bakhtin's notion is perhaps more useful in terms of discussing the generation of a text, Uspensky's in analyzing the resultant product. The former tends toward applying the reasoning processes of inductive thought, the latter would appear to afford a deductive counterpart.

10. Nonetheless, it also finds sympathetic resonance in the School's nascent studies of the semiotics of behavior (cf. Lotman and Uspensky 1984, 1985; Danow 1987b), to be further remarked.

11. The term 'text' itself does not appear rigorously defined. Attempts to grapple with the concept follow.

'Text may . . . be defined . . . [as] a concrete object having its own *internal* features which cannot be deduced from anything apart from itself' (Lotman and Piatigorsky 1978:233).

'A text is a separate message that is clearly perceived as being distinct from a "non-text" or "other text"'.

'A text has a beginning, end, and definite internal organization. An internal structure is inherent by definition in every text. An amorphous accumulation of signs is not a text' (Lotman 1977b:119). Conversely, a text is explicit in the sense that it is expressed according to a codified system of signs.

Concerning the ubiquity of texts, however, Lotman speaks with greater assurance, when he declares: 'We cannot point to a single human collective during the many centuries of man's history . . . which did not have texts and specialized behavior shown by certain people or by the entire collective at certain times to serve a particular cultural function' (Lotman 1976b:214).

7 Dialogic Poetics

1. Nonetheless, there may be a distinct communicative value in silence, explored most extensively as a literary strategy by Dostoevsky. For further discussion of this strategy, see Danow 1980.

2. Such contention does not overlook the fact that intonation in writing may be expressed in one way by means of italics.

This lack of a clear distinction between oral speech and the literary utterance is evidently noted later, when it is acknowledged: 'As, however, we do not have a gramophone record to give us a true record of conversation between living people, we have to make use of literary material, constantly, of course, taking account of its special, literary, character' (*MPL*, 130). The reference to a 'true record' of discourse as opposed to that 'special' character inherent in literary dialogue appears to accommodate the distinction between the literal and figurative.

3. The irony of buttressing an argument favoring a clear distinction between metaphorical and concrete usage by employing a common figurative expression is not lost here. In fact, its very employment goes a long way toward demonstrating how easily one may glide over the seeming bounds existing between the two.

Selected Bibliography

PRIMARY SOURCES

Bakhtin, Mikhail

1968 *Rabelais and his World*. Helene Iswolsky, trans. (Cambridge, Mass.: M.I.T. Press). [Orig. pub. 1965. Cited in the text as *RW*.]

1981 *The Dialogic Imagination; Four Essays by M.M. Bakhtin*. Michael Holquist, ed.; Caryl Emerson and Michael Holquist, trans. (Austin: University of Texas Press). [Essays of 1934–41; orig. pub. 1975. Cited as *DI*.]

1984 *Problems of Dostoevsky's Poetics*. Caryl Emerson, ed. and trans. (Minneapolis: University of Minnesota Press; Theory and History of Literature Series, Volume 8). [Orig. pub. 1929; revised 1963. Cited as *PDP*.]

1986 *Speech Genres and Other Late Essays*. Caryl Emerson and Michael Holquist, eds.; Vern W. McGee, trans. (Austin: University of Texas Press). [Essays and writings from 1940s through 1970s; orig. pub. 1979. Cited as *SG*.]

1990 *Art and Answerability; Early Philosophical Essays by M.M. Bakhtin*. Michael Holquist and Vadim Liapunov, eds.; Vadim Liapunov, trans. (Austin: University of Texas Press). [Essays of 1919–24; orig. pub. in 1975 and 1979. Cited as *Art*.]

Medvedev, P.N.

1978 *The Formal Method in Literary Scholarship; A Critical Introduction to Sociological Poetics*. Albert J. Wehrle, trans. (Baltimore: Johns Hopkins University Press). [Orig. pub. 1928. Cited as *FM*.]

1983 The Immediate Tasks Facing Literary–Historical Science. *Bakhtin School Papers*, Ann Shukman, ed. (Oxford: RPT Publications, Russian Poetics in Translation, No. 10), pp. 75–91. [Orig. pub. 1928. Cited as *BSP*.]

Voloshinov, V.N.

1973 *Marxism and the Philosophy of Language*. Ladislav Matejka and I.R. Titunik, trans. (New York: Seminar Press). [Orig. pub. 1929. Cited as *MPL*.]

1976 Discourse in Life and Discourse in Art (Concerning Sociological Poetics). *Freudianism: A Marxist Critique*. I.R. Titunik, trans. and ed. with Neal H. Bruss (New York: Academic Press), pp. 93–116. [Orig. pub. 1926. Cited as *Discourse*.]

1983 Literary Stylistics. *Bakhtin School Papers*, Ann Shukman, ed. (Oxford: RPT Publications; Russian Poetics in Translation, No. 10), pp. 93–152. [Orig. pub. 1930. Cited as *BSP*.]

SECONDARY SOURCES

Bernstein, Michael André

1983 When the Carnival Turns Bitter: Preliminary Reflections Upon the Abject Hero. *Critical Inquiry* 10 (2), 283–306.
1989 The Poetics of *Ressentiment*. *Rethinking Bakhtin; Extensions and Challenges*. Gary Saul Morson and Caryl Emerson, eds. (Evanston: Northwestern University Press), pp. 197–223.

Bialostosky, Don

1986 Dialogics as an Art of Discourse in Literary Criticism. *PMLA*, 101 (5), 788–97.

Booth, Wayne

1984 Introduction. *Problems of Dostoevsky's Poetics*, pp. xiii–xxvii.

Bové, Carol Mastrangelo

1983 The Text as Dialogue in Bakhtin and Kristeva. *The University of Ottawa Quarterly*, 53 (1), 117–24.

Champagne, Roland

1978 A Grammar of the Language of Culture: Literary Theory and Yury M. Lotman's Semiotics. *New Literary History* IX:2, 205–10.

Chernov, Igor

1988 Historical Survey of Tartu–Moscow Semiotic School. *Semiotics of Culture; Proceedings of the 25th Symposium of the Tartu–Moscow School of Semiotics, Imatra, Finland, 27th-29th July, 1987*, Henry Broms and Rebecca Kaufman, eds. (Helsinki: Arator Inc.), pp. 7–16.

Clark, Katerina and Michael Holquist

1984 *Mikhail Bakhtin*. (Cambridge: Harvard University Press).
1986 A Continuing Dialogue. *Slavic and East European Journal* 30 (1), 96–102.

Corredor, Eva

1983 Lukács and Bakhtin: A Dialogue on Fiction. *The University of Ottawa Quarterly*, 53 (1), 97–107.

Culler, Jonathan

1975 *Structuralist Poetics; Structuralism, Linguistics, and the Study of Literature.* (Ithaca: Cornell University Press).

Danow, David K

1980 Semiotics of Gesture in Dostoevskian Dialogue. *Russian Literature* 8 (1), 41–75.
1984 M.M. Bakhtin's Concept of the Word. *American Journal of Semiotics* 3 (1), 79–97.
1985 M.M. Bakhtin in Life and Art. *American Journal of Semiotics* 3 (3), 131–41.
1986 Temporal Strategies and Constraints in Narrative. *Semiotica* 58–3/4, 245–68.
1987a Literary Models and the Study of Narrative. *American Journal of Semiotics* 5 (3/4), 461–77.
1987b Lotman and Uspensky: A Perfusion of Models. *Semiotica* 64 (3/4), 343–57.
1988a Word, Utterance, Text. *Semiotica* 72 (1/2), 179–186.
1988b Dialogism: Perspectives and Delimitations. *Canadian-American Slavic Studies*, XXII (1–4), 43–50.
1988c Bakhtin and Lotman: Novel and Culture. *Semiotics of Culture; Proceedings of the 25th Symposium of the Tartu–Moscow School of Semiotics, Imatra, Finland, 27th-29th July, 1987*, Henri Broms and Rebecca Kaufman, eds. (Helsinki: Arator, Inc.), pp. 233–44.
1989a Sign and Spirit; The Semiotics of M.M. Bakhtin. *The Semiotic Web 1988*, Thomas A. Sebeok and Jean-Umiker Sebeok, eds. (Berlin, New York: Mouton de Gruyter), pp. 17–40.
1989b The Concept of Frame. *Working Papers and Pre-Publications*, Centro Internazionale di Semiotica e di Linguistica, Universita di Urbino, Number 189.
1991 The Legacy of M.M. Bakhtin. *Semiotica*, 83 (1/2).

DeJean, Joan

1984 Bakhtin and/in History. *Language and Literary Theory*. Benjamin A. Stolz, Lubomír Doležel, and I.R. Titunik, eds. (Ann Arbor: Papers in Slavic Philology, No. 5), pp. 225–40.

de Man, Paul

1983 Dialogue and Dialogism. *Poetics Today* 4 (1), 99–107.

Emerson, Caryl

1983a Translating Bakhtin: Does His Theory of Discourse Contain a Theory of Translation? *University of Ottawa Quarterly* 53 (1), 23–33.
1983b The Outer World and Inner Speech: Bakhtin, Vygotsky, and the Internalization of Language. *Critical Inquiry* 10 (2), 245–64.
1984 Editor's Preface. *Problems of Dostoevsky's Poetics*, pp. xxix–xliii.
1985 The Tolstoy Connection in Bakhtin. *PMLA*, 100 (1), 68–80.
1988 Problems with Baxtin's Poetics. *Slavic and East European Journal* 32 (4), 503–525.

Emerson, Caryl and Gary Saul Morson

1977 Penultimate Words. *The Current in Criticism: Essays on the Present and Future of Literary Theory*. Clayton Koelb and Virgil Lokke, eds (West Lafayette: Purdue University Press), pp. 43–64.

Fogel, Aaron

1989 Coerced Speech and the Oedipus Dialogue Complex. *Rethinking Bakhtin; Extensions and Challenges*. Gary Saul Morson and Caryl Emerson, eds (Evanston: Northwestern University Press), pp. 173–96.

Fokkema, D.W.

1976 Continuity and Change in Russian Formalism, Czech Structuralism, and Soviet Semiotics. *PTL: A Journal for Descriptive Poetics and Theory of Literature* 1, 153–96.

Forster, E.M.

1927 *Aspects of the Novel*. (New York: Harcourt, Brace and World).

Galan, F.W.

1985 *Historic Structures; The Prague School Project, 1928–1946*. (Austin: University of Texas Press).

Hirschkop, Ken

1985 The Social and the Subject in Bakhtin. *Poetics Today*, 6 (4), 769–75.
1986 Bakhtin, Discourse and Democracy. *New Left Review*, 160, 92–113.

Hirschkop, Ken and David Shepherd

1989 *Bakhtin and Cultural Theory* (Manchester and New York: Manchester University Press).

Holquist, Michael

1981a Introduction. *The Dialogic Imagination*, pp. xiii–xxxiv.
1981b The Politics of Representation. *Allegory and Representation*. Stephen J. Greenblatt, ed. (Baltimore: Johns Hopkins University Press), pp. 162–83.
1982 "Bad Faith" Squared: The Case of M.M. Bakhtin. *Russian Literature and Criticism; Selected Papers from the Second World Congress for Soviet and East European Studies*. Evelyn Bristol, ed. (Berkeley: Berkeley Slavic Specialties), pp. 214–34.
1983 Answering as Authoring: Mikhail Bakhtin's Trans-Linguistics. *Critical Inquiry* 10 (2), 307–19.
1985 Bakhtin and the Formalists; History as Dialogue. *Russian Formalism: A Retrospective Glance*. Robert Louis Jackson and Stephen Rudy, eds. (New Haven: Yale Center for International and Area Studies), pp. 82–95.
1986 Introduction. *Speech Genres and Other Late Essays*, pp. ix–xxiii.

Ivanov, Viach. Vs.

1974 The Significance of M.M. Bakhtin's Ideas on Sign, Utterance, and Dialogue for Modern Semiotics. *Semiotics and Structuralism*. Henryk Baran, ed. (White Plains, New York: International Arts and Sciences Press), pp. 310–67. [Orig. pub. 1973]

Jakobson, Roman and Jurij Tynjanov

1971 Problems in the Study of Language and Literature. *Readings in Russian Poetics: Formalist and Structuralist Views*. Ladislav Matejka and Krystyna Pomorska, eds (Cambridge, Mass.: M.I.T. press), pp. 79–81. [Orig. pub. 1928]

Kozhinov, Vadim

1977 The World of M.M. Bakhtin. *Soviet Literature*, 1, pp. 143–4.

Kristeva, Julia

1972 The Ruin of a Poetics. *Twentieth Century Studies; Russian Formalism* 7/8. Stephen Bann and John E. Bowlt, eds. (Edinburgh: Scottish Academic press), pp. 102–19. [Orig. pub. 1970]
1980 Word, Dialogue, and Novel. *Desire in Language; A Semiotic Approach to Literature and Art*. Leon S. Roudiez, ed.; Thomas Gora, Alice Jardine, and Leon S. Roudiez, trans. (New York: Columbia University Press), pp. 64–91. [Orig. pub. 1967]

Lotman, Ju. M. (Yu. M./Jurij)

1974 The Sign Mechanism of Culture. *Semiotica* 12:4, 301–5. [Orig. pub. 1973]

1976a The Modeling Significance of the Concepts 'End' and 'Beginning' in Artistic Texts. *General Semiotics*, Ann Shukman, ed. (Oxford: RPT Publications; Russian Poetics in Translation, No. 3), pp. 7–11.

1976b Culture and Information. *Dispositio* 1 (3), 213–15. [Orig. pub. 1970]

1977a *The Structure of the Artistic Text*. Ronald Vroon, trans. (Ann Arbor: Michigan Slavic Contributions No. 7). [orig. pub. 1970]

1977b Problems in the Typology of Texts. *Soviet Semiotics; An Anthology*. Daniel P. Lucid, ed. (Baltimore and London: The Johns Hopkins University Press), pp. 119–24. [Orig. pub. 1966]

1977c The Dynamic Model of a Semiotic System. *Semiotica* 21:3/4, 193–210. [Orig. pub. 1974]

1977d Two Models of Communication. *Soviet Semiotics; An Anthology*. Daniel P. Lucid, ed. (Baltimore and London: The Johns Hopkins University Press), pp. 99–101. [Orig. pub. 1970]

Lotman, Yu. M. and A.M. Piatigorsky

1978 Text and Function. *New Literary History* IX:2, 233–44. [Orig. pub. 1968]

Lotman, Yu. M. and B.A. Uspensky

1978 On the Semiotic Mechanism of Culture. *New Literary History* IX:2, 211–32. [Orig. pub. 1971]

1984 *The Semiotics of Russian Culture* (=Michigan Slavic Contributions, No. 11), Ann Shukman (ed.). Ann Arbor: Michigan Slavic Publications.

1985 *The Semiotics of Russian Cultural History*, Alexander and Alice Nakhimovsky (eds). Ithaca: Cornell University Press.

Lotman, Ju. M., et al.

1975 Theses on the Semiotic Study of Cultures (as Applied to Slavic Texts). *The Tell-Tale Sign; A Survey of Semiotics*. Thomas A. Sebeok, ed. (Lisse: Peter de Ridder Press, 1975), pp. 57–83. [Orig. pub. 1973]

Lukács, Georg

1971 *The Theory of the Novel* (Cambridge, Mass.: M.I.T. Press).

Matejka, Ladislav

1973   On the First Russian Prolegomena to Semiotics. *Marxism and the Philosophy of Language,* pp. 161–74.
1976   Postscript. Prague School Semiotics. *Semiotics of Art: Prague School Contributions.* Ladislav Matejka and Irwin R. Titunik, eds (Cambridge, Mass.: M.I.T. Press), pp. 265–90.

Matejka, Ladislav and Krystyna Pomorska

1971   *Readings in Russian Poetics: Formalist and Structuralist Views* (Cambridge, Mass.: M.I.T. Press).

McHale, Brian

1978   Free Indirect Discourse: A Survey of Recent Accounts. *PTL: A Journal for Descriptive Poetics and Theory of Literature* 3, 249–87.

Morson, Gary Saul

1978   The Heresiarch of *META. PTL: A Journal for Descriptive Poetics and Theory of Literature* 3, 407–27.
1981   Tolstoy's Absolute Language. *Critical Inquiry,* VII (4), pp. 667–87.
1983   Who Speaks for Bakhtin?: A Dialogic Introduction. *Critical Inquiry* 10 (2), 225–43.
1986a *Bakhtin: Essays and Dialogues on His Work.* (Chicago and London: University of Chicago Press).
1986b The Baxtin Industry. *Slavic and East European Journal* 30 (1), 81–90.

Morson, Gary Saul and Caryl Emerson

1989   *Rethinking Bakhtin; Extensions and Challenges.* (Evanston: Northwestern University Press).

Mukařovský, Jan

1970   *Aesthetic Function, Norm and Value as Social Facts.* Mark E. Suino, trans. (Ann Arbor: Michigan Slavic Contributions No. 3). [Orig. pub. 1936]
1976   Poetic Reference. *Semiotics of Art: Prague School Contributions.* Ladislav Matejka and Irwin R. Titunik, eds (Cambridge, Mass.: M.I.T. Press), pp. 155–63. [Orig. pub. 1936]
1977   *The Word and Verbal Art; Selected Essays by Jan Mukařovský.* John Burbank and Peter Steiner, trans. and eds (New Haven and London: Yale University Press).
1978   *Structure, Sign, and Function; Selected Essays by Jan Mukařovský.* John Burbank and Peter Steiner, trans. and eds (New Haven and London: Yale University Press).

1982 Structuralism in Esthetics and in Literary Studies. *The Prague School; Selected Writings, 1929–1946.* Peter Steiner, ed. (Austin: University of Texas Press), pp. 65–82. [Orig. pub. 1941; revised 1948]

Mukařovský, et al. (The Prague Linguistic Circle)

1982 Theses Presented to the First Congress of Slavic Philologists. *The Prague School; Selected Writings, 1929–1946.* Peter Steiner, ed. (Austin: University of Texas Press), pp. 3–31. [Orig. pub. 1929]

Parrott, Ray

1984 (Re)capitulation, Parody or Polemic? *Language and Literary Theory.* Benjamin A. Stolz, I.R. Titunik, and Lubomír Doležel, eds (Ann Arbor: Papers in Slavic Philology, No. 5), pp. 463–88.

Patterson, David

1985 Mikhail Bakhtin and the Dialogical Discussion of the Novel. *Journal of Aesthetics and Art Criticism,* XLIV (2), 131–8.
1988 *Literature and Spirit; Essays on Bakhtin and His Contemporaries.* (Lexington: University of Kentucky Press).

Perlina, Nina

1983 Bakhtin – Medvedev – Voloshinov: An Apple of Discourse. *University of Ottawa Quarterly* 53 (1), 35–47.
1985 *Varieties of Poetic Utterance.* (Lanham: University Press of America).

Peirce, Charles Sanders

1933 *Logic and Mathematics* in *The Collected Papers of Charles Sanders Peirce,* Vol. IV. Charles Hartshorne and Paul Weiss, eds (Cambridge, Mass.: Harvard University Press).
1935 *Ontology and Cosmology* in *The Collected Papers of Charles Sanders Peirce,* Vol. VI. Charles Hartshorne and Paul Weiss, eds (Cambridge, Mass.: Harvard University Press).

Pomorska, Krystyna

1978 Mikhail Bakhtin and His Verbal Universe. *PTL,* III, 379–86.

Segal, Dmitri

1974 *Aspects of Structuralism in Soviet Philology, Papers on Poetics and Semiotics,* 2, Department of Poetics and Comparative Literature, Tel-Aviv University, Tel-Aviv.

Shukman, Ann

1976   *Literature and Semiotics: A Study of the Writings of Yu. M. Lotman.*
        (Amsterdam: North Holland Press).
1977   Jurij Lotman and the Semiotics of Culture. *Russian Literature* 5:1,
        41–53.
1980   Between Marxism and Formalism: The Stylistics of Mikhail Bakh-
        tin. *Comparative Criticism; A Yearbook,* Eleanor Shaffer, ed., pp.
        221–34.
1983   Editor's Introduction. *Bakhtin School Papers,* pp. 1–4.
1984   Bakhtin and Tolstoy. *Studies in Twentieth Century Literature,* IX
        (1), 57–74.

Silverman, David and Brian Torode

1980   *The Material Word: Some Theories of Language and Its Limits.* (Lon-
        don and Boston), pp. 305–10.

Steiner, Peter

1978   Jan Mukařovský's Structural Aesthetics. *Structure, Sign, and
        Function; Selected Essays by Jan Mukařovský.* John Burbank and
        Peter Steiner, trans. and eds (New Haven and London: Yale
        University Press), pp. ix-xxxix.
1982   The Roots of Structuralist Esthetics. *The Prague School; Selected
        Writings, 1929–1946.* Peter Steiner, ed. (Austin: University of
        Texas Press), pp. 174–219.

Stewart, Susan

1983   Shouts on the Street: Bakhtin's Anti-Linguistics. *Critical Inquiry*
        10 (2), 265–82.

Thomson, Clive

1983   The Semiotics of M.M. Bakhtin. *University of Ottawa Quarterly* 53
        (1), 11–22.
1984   Bakhtin's 'Theory' of Genre. *Studies in Twentieth Century Litera-
        ture,* IX (1), 29–40.

Titunik, I.R.

1973   The Formal Method and the Sociological Method (M.M. Baxtin,
        P.N. Medvedev, V.N. Vološinov) in Russian Theory and Study
        of Literature. *Marxism and the Philosophy of Language,* pp. 175–200.
1976   M.M. Baxtin (The Baxtin School) and Soviet Semiotics. *Dispositio*
        1 (3), 327–38.
1984   Bakhtin &/or Voloshinov &/or Medvedev: Dialogue &/or Double-
        talk? *Language and Literary Theory.* Benjamin A. Stolz, I.R. Titunik,

and Lubomír Doležel, eds (Ann Arbor: Papers in Slavic Philology, No. 5), pp. 535–64.

1986 The Baxtin Problem: Concerning Katerina Clark and Michael Holquist's *Mikhail Bakhtin. Slavic and East European Journal* 30 (1), 91–5.

Todorov, Tzvetan

1984 *Mikhail Bakhtin: The Dialogical Principle.* Wlad Godzich, trans. (Minneapolis: University of Minnesota Press; Theory and History of Literature Series, Volume 13).

Uspensky, Boris

1973 *A Poetics of Composition; The Structure of the Artistic Text and Typology of a Compositional Form.* Valentina Zavarin and Susan Wittig, trans. (Berkeley and Los Angeles: University of California Press).

Wehrle, Albert

1978 Introduction: M.M. Bakhtin/P.N. Medvedev. *The Formal Method in Literary Scholarship*, pp. ix–xxiii.

Veltruský, Jiří

1981 Jan Mukařovský's Structural Poetics and Esthetics. *Poetics Today* 2:1b, 117–57.
1984 Semiotic Notes on Dialogue in Literature. *Language and Literary Theory*, eds Benjamin A. Stolz, I.R. Titunik, and Lubomír Doležel (Ann Arbor: Papers in Slavic Philology, No. 5), pp. 595–607.

Winner, Irene Portis

1979 Ethnicity, Modernity, and Theory of Culture Texts. *Semiotics of Culture.* Thomas A. Sebeok, ed. (The Hague: Mouton), pp. 103–47.

Winner, Irene and Thomas Winner

1976 The Semiotics of Cultural Texts. *Semiotica* 18:2, 101–56.

Winner, Thomas

1973 The Aesthetics and Poetics of the Prague Linguistic Circle. *Poetica* 8, 77–96.
1976 Jan Mukařovský: The Beginnings of Structural and Semiotic Aesthetics. *Sound, Sign and Meaning: Quinquagenary of the Prague*

Linguistic Circle. Ladislav Matejka, ed. (Ann Arbor: Michigan Slavic Contributions No. 6), pp. 433–55.

1978 On the Relation of Verbal and Nonverbal Art in Early Prague Semiotics: Jan Mukařovský. *The Sign; Semiotics Around the World.* R.W. Bailey, L. Matejka and P. Steiner, eds (Ann Arbor: Michigan Slavic Contributions No. 9), pp. 227–37.

Index